The Afterlife

The Revd John Spooner was ordained in 1989 and is currently Honorary Chaplain to St James Healing Ministry. He has previously lectured in travel and tourism and worked with Qantas for ten years. He was awarded an M.A. with Merit by Sydney University for his study of the early church in New South Wales. This is his fourth book.

Previous books

The Golden See: A History of the Anglican Diocese of Ballarat

The Archbishops of Railway Square: A History of Christ Church, St. Laurence, Sydney

Only Luke is With Me

The Afterlife

THE EVIDENCE OF NEAR DEATH EXPERIENCES

The Revd John William Dubois Spooner;
MA, BD, Dip. Ed.
Hon. Chaplain St. James, Healing Ministry

HALSTEAD PRESS

SYDNEY MMXVI
Published by Halstead Press
Unit 66, 89–97 Jones Street
Ultimo, New South Wales, 2007

and

Gorman House, Ainslie Avenue
Braddon, Australian Capital Territory, 2612

 Designed by Kylie Maxwell, ePrintDesign. Printed by Ligare in Sydney.

National Library cataloguing-in-publication entry

Creator: Spooner, John, 1929-, author.
Title: The afterlife : the evidence of near death experiences / John Spooner.
ISBN: 9781925043310 (paperback)
Subjects: Future life
Near-death experiences.

Dewey Number: 236.2

Contents

Epitaph

I have been to that heaven where His light
Beams brightest, and seen things that none, returning,
Has the knowledge or the power to repeat,
Because, as it draws near to its desire,
Our intellect sinks down to such a depth
That memory cannot trace its way back there.

Dante Alighieri (c.1265–c.1321)

CHAPTER 1

Introduction

As a Christian minister of religion, I stood beside an open grave recently, prior to a committal, and recited, as is my wont on such occasions, the words of the 23rd Psalm: "Though I walk through the valley of the shadow of death, I will fear no evil: for thou art with me." How often I have thought of them and spoken them, not only at committals but, even more importantly, at the bedside of the dying about to make their leap into the great unknown.

But is it a "great unknown"? A study of near death experiences (NDEs) suggests otherwise. There is now a considerable literature in the form of reports made by people who have experienced one, and an objective study of the evidence of these near death experiencers is most revealing.

How does such an experience fit with religious faith? For me this is important, as many of my fellow clergy, along with many in the medical profession, are amongst the greatest sceptics about the reality of NDEs. Essentially their argument is: "Oh, but that's not something we learned in theological college." Or, "There's nothing about that in the Bible."

But indeed there is.

My experience of an NDE, at age of five, was limited, but enough to make me inquisitive for the rest of my life, and to be a contributing factor in my eventual ordination to priestly Anglican ministry, and to becoming a member of the International Association of Near-Death Studies (IANDS).

As a small boy I faced serious abdominal surgery. But my distress, on the morning the operation was scheduled, was such that I heard the surgeon say that he hesitated to proceed. Instead he asked for my mother to be sent for (those were less enlightened days when loved ones, even of small children, were kept waiting outside). She came, sat by my side and stroked my forehead. Soon I was overcome by an overwhelming sense of peace, and ever since I have known the meaning of the biblical "peace of God which passes all understanding", reportedly experienced by many near death experiencers. She was more than a mother that day, she was a medium of God's love.

The surgeon, seeing my changed state, invited the anaesthetist to proceed, while allowing my mother to continue to sit beside me. He commenced and I found myself being drawn, in a whirling sensation, down a dark tunnel—something which I can remember eighty-three years later with great clarity—but there was no fear. That was the end of the experience and the next I knew I was awake and recovering from what proved to be successful surgery.

But the experience of other people has been just as important, particularly what I learned from a 4 a.m. interview on the Monday morning of a long weekend on ABC radio, which I had reluctantly agreed to following my return from the annual convention of International Association of Near-Death Studies in North America. During the interview I referred to the many speakers who came to the convention from many different parts of the world, wanting to talk about their NDEs.

They came at their own considerable expense, and had nothing to gain except the rare opportunity to talk to a sympathetic audience. They knew they would not be patronised as they had when endeavouring to talk about their experiences to doctors, ministers of religion, or even close family. "Drugs", "hallucination" and "bad dream" were the type of explanation they were offered, whereas they knew it in some cases, more than fifty years on, to be the most profound and real experience of their lives.

I spoke for about fifteen minutes and for the rest of the hour invited the audience—(if there was one, I thought at 4 a.m.)—to call if they had had an NDE. The switchboard lit up like a birthday cake with fifty candles and I was overwhelmed by callers. The most common theme was that they had never been able to talk about this before for fear of being patronised or even ridiculed. On arrival home from the ABC studio at 6 a.m., having suggested to callers who had been unable to get through that they send me an e-mail, I found my computer full of messages.

Most significantly in relation to the title of this book, I learned from many of them, as I had from the conference delegates, that they will never fear death again.

My conviction concerning the life to come, or afterlife, is that there is no death, only transformation[1]—a view not limited to Christians, nor shared by all other Christian ministers.

I believe in transition to a higher life, but in order to inherit that higher form of life we have to discard our old form, our body, just as the butterfly had to discard its previous body of a caterpillar in order to inherit the sky. And just as a seemingly dead seed must be buried in the ground for even more beautiful life to spring forth, so we too will be given a new form while remaining the same you and I, the same unique personalities.

A personality as unique as our fingerprints. Like the butterfly, changed, but not changed.

Raison d'être

That an afterlife exists and that NDEs are real experiences providing glimpses into that afterlife, is something I cannot prove—so why should I be writing a book such as this? It is because I believe them, and wish to state a case for their reality and in writing, to share that great hope I have with others.

Why? Because there is no greater issue for all of us than death—whatever our belief or unbelief.

If God is, then He must be God of all creation not just Christians. You will hear from me again a statement from an anonymous source which I have long embraced "there is only one God, but He has many different names." Think for yourself of those various names. One God, but many different names.

If God is, and He is love, as Christians and many near death experiencers insist, then death is not the end, for a loving God is not a God who creates just to destroy.

CHAPTER 2

Belief in an Afterlife

The Anglican Archbishop of Sydney said in his 2016 Easter Day sermon, "Death is our enemy. Death is not natural to this world . . . it is not the way God made the world when everything was good. Regardless of how much money you've accumulated, how many friends you have won, how much fame and fortune you might have . . . death will meet you at the end." [*Sydney Morning Herald*, 28 March 2016]

Indeed that is so, but is death to this life the end? To explore that question let us first confirm the Christian position, proclaimed of course by the archbishop, then that of other religions.

The Christian position on an afterlife is based on Jesus' own words—that he goes to prepare a place for us, and to the thief dying on the Cross next to him that this day he, the thief, will be in paradise with him. But Jesus says very little about the nature of that life to come, and tells his disciples at one stage, who desire to know more, that they have not yet fully understood what he has tried to teach them about this life. In other words they are not yet ready for deeper knowledge.

And it is in this context that an investigation of near death experiences, as to whether they are "real" and not hallucinatory, is undertaken. If real do they shed light on the nature of the afterlife? Do they provide us with deeper knowledge?

It is in this context that I explore the great hope and belief in an afterlife first by different religions, then confirming the Christian position, finally by investigating near death experiences, if real and not imaginary, as to what light they may shed on the nature of that afterlife. Pursuing the possible relevance of near death experiences to an afterlife is pointless without first endeavouring to establish the reality or otherwise of an afterlife.

The crucial point for me has always been this: Is a near death experience evidence that life is unbroken by physical death? Because the classic NDE only makes sense if that is so.

A good starting point is what C.S. Lewis said of Jesus' claims about Himself which figure prominently in the gospels, particularly in St. John's, often known as the 'I Am' gospel. Lewis said he could only see three alternatives about Jesus: Jesus was a liar, or was mad, or was who he said He was, the Son of God.

Believing the latter, I then turn to what Jesus had to say about the subject of continuing life.

Which seems unequivocal.

First and most telling, His story about Dives and Lazarus (Luke 16:19–31), the rich man and the poor man who both die and the different states in which they find themselves on the other side of death. The poor man who had sat begging at the rich man's gate is gathered into "Abraham's bosom", but not Dives, who finds himself in such miserable circumstances that he asks to be allowed to return to earth to warn his brothers about the consequences of the selfish life which he and they had led. He is denied, having crossed the barrier which many near death experiencers record; and over which if they were to cross there could be no return to this life.

Then His words to His disciples as He was leaving them: "In my Father's house there are many rooms, I go to prepare a place for you that where I am you may be also. If it were not so would I not have told you?" (John 14:2)

Again, the story in the gospels of His transfiguration on Mount Tabor, where Peter, James, and John record Him talking with Moses and Elijah who had been "dead" for hundreds of years; at which time Jesus explains that God "is not God of the dead, but God of the living."[2]

Finally, Jesus' words to the penitent thief dying on the cross next to Him: "Verily, verily, I tell you this day you will be with me in paradise." (Luke 23:43)

Not in fifty millennia when somebody blows a big trumpet, but this day.

These episodes should be sufficient evidence, especially for Christians, that death is not the end, that life does continue beyond the grave. In what follows, we will look at commonly reported experiences of classic near death experiences to see if there is any conflict with, not only what Christians believe—but also with those of other religious faiths, and of agnostics and atheists.

Finally, why should I, one who has never had a full-blown NDE, be writing this work? It is because of the profound belief I have in the life of the world to come, a belief that, for me as a Christian, is based upon Jesus' own words. I would like to share with as many as possible, religious or not, my conviction that the tragedies and disasters of this life—the "where is God?" question of so many, the best example of which is surely Auschwitz?—can only make some sense within the context of life being eternal and involving justice, as so beautifully expressed by Mother Julian of Norwich: "All shall be well and all manner of things shall be well."

My purpose therefore is to present a case for the afterlife as a reality based on Christian belief, along with the beliefs of people of other faiths, using the revelations within near death experiences as major evidence in support.

And to develop that case, one must also consider the attitude of non-Christians, people of different religious faiths, and people of no faith, the disinterested, atheists and agnostics.

MAJOR RELIGIONS

It appears that belief in an afterlife among mainstream religions is near universal. The following is a summary of their beliefs.[3]

1. **Mainstream Christianity:** Enshrined in the Nicene Creed, the credal standard-bearer of the Christian faith: "We believe in the resurrection of the dead and the life of the world to come." A more positive statement could not be made, one affirmed daily throughout the Christian world.

2. **Seventh Day Adventists** accept the Sleep Theory—that until the second coming of Christ, the redeemed stay "asleep", but then are resurrected to eternal life.
3. **Mormons:** There is a spirit world in which the dead remain until judgement.
4. **Islam:** There are two places, Jannat (Paradise) and Jahannam (Hell), where the dead will remain until judgement day. After an interval in the grave the dead will be raised by summoning angels.
5. **Judaism:** Sheol is the place of the dead. Orthodox Jews maintain a belief in bodily resurrection as with Christians, but most Reform Jews are only "concerned with spiritual survival."[4]
6. **Hinduism,** on one hand sees an afterlife as a drop merging with an ocean, on the other as a personal relation with the object of devotion in this life. Nevertheless for both positions,[5] "rebirth has become an evil to be brought to an end."
7. **Buddhism:** Reincarnation, or even being reborn as an animal.[6]

The general acceptance of an afterlife amongst religious groups does not rule out the possibility of the afterlife being mere optimism—an "emotional crutch", as many critics claim—which needs to be addressed. I think of my own experience and, I must admit, there are times when my faith has been low that I have asked myself: "Do I believe because I believe, or do I believe because I want to believe?"

The following is the attitude of some other groups and individuals:

AGNOSTICISM

Agnostics hold that the truth of claims about the existence or non-existence of any deity, as well as other religious claims, is unknowable.

Agnosticism can be defined in various ways. In some senses, agnosticism is a stance about the difference between belief and knowledge, rather than about any specific claim or belief. In the popular sense, an

> agnostic is someone who neither believes nor disbelieves in the existence of a deity or deities, whereas a theist and an atheist believe and disbelieve, respectively. In the strict sense, however, agnosticism is the view that humanity does not currently possess the requisite knowledge and/or reason to provide sufficient rational grounds to justify the belief that deities either do or do not exist.

Which view, of course, includes belief or non-belief in an afterlife. It is not a denial, but in simple terms: *"I don't know."*

ATHEISM

Just as religious views about an afterlife do not prove anything, merely stating a belief and reasons for it, so too does the atheistic view fail to prove anything, but it is nevertheless important to know the opinion of such a significant cross-section of the community.

A leading authority[7] expresses their answer to the question of what they believe about an afterlife this way:

> Put simply . . . nothing. When the body dies, the brain ceases to function. At that moment all of your thoughts, feelings, memories, and emotions cease to exist.
>
> As we do not believe in a soul, we do not believe that any of these things survive beyond the moment of death. There is simply no evidence in reality to believe that some form of mystical entity known as the "soul" somehow exits the body and moves to another plane or dimension of existence. . . also for which there is no evidence.

AIR CHIEF MARSHALL, LORD DOWDING

One particularly interesting, and as far as I know unique, view of the afterlife is that of Lord Dowding, expressed in his book *Many Mansions*—although some might see his claims as fanciful. Dowding was a complex man. He was a fighter pilot in World War I, the head of RAF Fighter Command in the Battle of Britain in 1940, a champion skier, a spiritualist, a vegetarian, and a believer in fairies!

His claims about the nature of the afterlife are based upon

information given to him by spiritualists, psychic mediums who claim communication with the dead from soldiers who had been killed in the First World War.

Many elements of NDEs appear in his book, such as encounters with a being of light, but it is the essence of that afterlife which is most interesting. Dowding posits that life can be seen as a progression through a series of spheres inside of each other. The outer sphere is the life in which we presently live and is the starting point of the afterlife from which one "graduates" to the next sphere, the peeling of an onion so to speak, a progression of spiritual growth that continues until the final stage of entering into the inner core, the presence of God.

Some sceptics might see his claims as fanciful, even fraudulent, but whatever one's attitude to his claim that they come from the "dead" via mediums, he cannot be dismissed lightly considering his reputation as affirmed on his statue standing outside St. Clement Danes Church on the Strand, London's most prominent street, connecting the West End to the City:

> Air Chief Marshal Lord Dowding was commander-in-chief of Fighter Command, Royal Air Force, from its formation in 1936 until November 1940. He was thus responsible for the preparation for and the conduct of the Battle of Britain. With remarkable foresight, he ensured the equipment of his command with monoplane fighters, the Hurricane and the Spitfire. He was among the first to appreciate the vital importance of R.D.F. (radar) and an effective command and control system for his squadrons. They were ready when war came.
>
> In the preliminary stages of that war, he thoroughly trained his minimal forces and conserved them against strong political pressure to disperse and misuse them. His wise and prudent judgement and leadership helped to ensure victory against overwhelming odds and thus prevented the loss of the Battle of Britain and probably the whole war.
>
> To him, the people of Britain and of the Free World owe largely the way of life and the liberties they enjoy today.

His stated claims about the nature of the afterlife may have made him a victim of fraud by his sources, but it is difficult to regard such a man as he himself fraudulent. Gullible perhaps, but not fraudulent.

TIBETAN BUDDHIST VIEW

Sogyal Rinpoche, born in Tibet, is a Buddhist, but has had wide exposure to Western, and in particular Christian, culture. In his well-known book, *The Tibetan Book of the Living and Dying*, he writes that when he first came to the West he was shocked by the contrast between the attitudes to death that he had been brought up with and those he had then found. He claims that modern Western society, for all its technological achievements, has no real understanding of death or what happens after death, and offers a detailed account of the Buddhist belief in the afterlife, and its nature.

DINESH D'SOUZA[8]

D'Souza is a co-founder and director of the Y Institute, a former Reagan and White House policy analyst. He has been a fellow at the American Enterprise Institute, the Hoover Institution at Stanford University. He is the author of several bestselling books including *What's So Great About Christianity*. His works are highly recommended reading for those who wish to know more about the afterlife and near death experiences.

He offers the following insights into the afterlife:

> Across the cultures of the world, both East and West, and right through the long march of history, people have affirmed that this life is one chapter in a larger story of existence, and that there is life after death.
>
> We think of this attitude as religious, fostered by the clergy, and for the most part it was. Many of the world's greatest scientists and philosophers however, from Socrates to Galileo to John Locke to Isaac Newton, also affirmed their belief in the afterlife. Even sceptical Enlightenment figures such as Thomas Paine, Thomas Jefferson, and Benjamin Franklin professed similar views. Europe is the only continent where a bare majority of people believe in the afterlife. By comparison nearly 80% of Americans today affirm life after death, and the percentage is even higher, in fact close to 100%, in non-Western cultures.

SO CALLED "PRIMITIVE PEOPLE"

An author of note, Harry Fosdick, argues that among all primitive people, the abode of the dead was definitely imagined, and from that place of shadows the friends who had gone came back in dreams to warn and counsel their descendants.[9]

To the native North Americans, the abode of the dead was a happy hunting ground away in the west; to the Maori of New Zealand it lay at the base of a great precipice; for the Finns and Australians, the dead inhabited a distant island; the Polynesians, that they dwelt in the Moon; the Mexicans and the Peruvians, in the sun; and the most popular idea of all, amongst Teutons, Egyptians, Greeks, Romans and Hebrews the destination of the dying was a subterranean cavern, from which mysterious, well guarded passages led to the surface of the earth.

Fosdick also said, quoting Max Muller in the 19th century, that even the "lowest savages" now living possess words for body and for soul;

> If we take the Tasmanians, a recently extinct race of savages, we find that however much different observers may contradict each other as to their intellectual faculties, they all agree that they have names for soul; nay that they all believe in the immortality of the soul.[10]

BENJAMIN FRANKLIN: SCIENTIST, INVENTOR, WRITER (1706–90)

> You desire to know something of my religion . . . here is my Creed. I believe in one God, Creator of the universe. That he governs it by his Providence, that he ought to be worshipped, that the most acceptable service we render to him is doing good to his other children. That the soul of man is immortal and will be treated with justice in another life respecting its conduct in this.[11]

WISHFUL THINKING?

So many believers, but how much is wishful thinking? How much does it conform with my admission—me, a Christian priest—of times of doubt when I ask "Do I believe because I believe or do I believe because I want to believe?" D'Souza goes on to give a reasoned rational argument to rebut the wishful thinking argument, which will be pursued.

If we accept as reasonable that the afterlife is a probability rather than a possibility we may ask is there evidence to substantiate such a claim? I will argue that such evidence can be found in the revelations of people who have had a near death experience, justifying my use of NDEs as "real" experiences as consistently asserted by the experiencers themselves, rather than hallucinatory, imaginative, or drug induced experiences.

WHAT DOES CHRISTIAN DOCTRINE SAY ABOUT AN AFTERLIFE?

In several places in the New Testament we find the notion that the dead are consciously dwelling somewhere awaiting final judgement. Some of the best known references to an afterlife include John 14:2–3 where Jesus is quoted as saying that there are many mansions in God's house and that he is leaving his followers "to prepare a place for you, that where I am you may be also"; Matthew 6:20, referring to earthly riches: "lay up for yourselves treasures in heaven, where neither moth nor rust doth corrupt, and where thieves do not break through"; Luke 23:43 where Jesus says to the thief dying on the cross next to him "this day you will be with me in paradise".

The phrase "eternal life" appears many times in the New Testament, and on most occasions it is referred to in the present tense suggesting it is something we already have. Indeed, it can be argued that unless that is so, it is a contradiction in terms. For example, John 3:3: "He who believes in the Son has eternal life." Therefore, afterlife should not be seen as a contradiction of eternal life, but rather as the next stage in the unbroken progress of eternal life.

John 5:13 defines eternal life as something the Christian, through his belief, has already been given by God. John 3:15–16; John 3:36; John 4:41; John 5:24 define how one obtains eternal life, viz., belief in Jesus as the Son of God.

But it also invites the question: Rather than eternal life being a gift to be bestowed on judgement day may it be a gift to be taken away?

An early commentator on Christian belief in an afterlife, Giovanni Papini refers to the First Epistle of Peter in the New Testament, saying that after the glad tidings of his resurrection Jesus then took the message to the dead, "who for untold ages had been waiting for this day in the depths of Sheol", and refers to the dead as: "They who had prophesied without knowing his name, and for whom they had waited in Sheol."[12]

Two events in particular concerning the afterlife, involving statements by Jesus, are the Ascension and his story referred to earlier of Dives and Lazarus. In the Ascension is found the Christian teaching that the resurrected Jesus was taken up into heaven in the presence of three of His apostles.

But the most telling, for a Christian, is that story of Dives and Lazarus—in which, it is critical to note, as Jesus tells it, there is no break in life, that for Dives and Lazarus there was no loss of identity, they were still the same persons, the same personalities as in their earthly life with clear recollections of that life.

Why would Jesus tell such a story of continuing life beyond the grave if the essence of it were not true?

Some contend it is only a parable, but that is semantics. Such a story would be consistent with Lewis' alternatives of Him being mad or a liar, but not if He was who He said He was.

And Matthew 10:28 is particularly relevant to Christian doctrinal teaching that people should not be afraid of people who want to kill them, saying that "they can only kill your body, but cannot touch your soul." Acts 2:27 and Revelation 20:4 also suggest the survival of the soul following physical death.

INSIGHT VERSUS SIGHT

Perhaps the most familiar difficulty in belief in eternal life is that appearances are against it. Fosdick, however, argues a powerful case against appearances, a case for insight against sight:

> Whoever has seen a person grow gradually old, mind failing as body drooped, until the mind a blank, understands the argument of appearance against immortality. All that we can see dies . . . our eyes bear witness to the dead and crumbling body, our ears bear witness to the fact that the voice is still . . . all our senses rise up and cry that our friend has perished. For most this simple fact is the greatest single difficulty in the way of faith. But this obstacle however is manifestly inconclusive.
>
> If we were to live by looks we should live in grossest ignorance of all the most important facts, not only of the spiritual but of the physical world. The sun looks as though it were moving, but it is not; the earth looks as though it were flat when it is round, and as though it were standing still when it is moving at over a thousand miles a minute; at noon the stars appear to be gone but they are there; put a straight stick in a calm pool and it appears to be crooked while it is still straight; sight says that a man grows smaller as he recedes into distance but insight says he does not; insight perceives governing laws dominant and irreversible. Sight sees a flat earth circled by planets, but insight knows that all the looks are false.
>
> The truth of immortality is a matter of thought, not of appearance, of reason, not of looks; the organ of perception fitted to deal with immortality is the mind not the eye. Looks therefore are an utterly inconclusive argument, and the person who disbelieves immortality because of appearances is essentially in the same intellectual class as the young child, who after the fashion of Alice in Wonderland, supposes that folks really grow small or large in proportion to their distance from the eye of the beholder because it looks that way. [13]

But Christians need no special insights as the afterlife has the authority of Jesus Himself. However, please note that I do not suggest that eternal life is exclusively for Christians. How unjust that would be. Think of unbaptised babies, or people of other cultures who have never heard the Christian gospel, such as all those still-to-be-discovered tribes in the highlands of Papua New Guinea. Or even prison inmates in our own society who have never known anything else in their upbringing other than violence, murder, incest, rape, and drug abuse . . . have they ever really had the opportunity to accept or reject the gospel which most of them have never had exposure to?

What matters, therefore, is not to focus upon Christian affiliation, but who Jesus speaks up for (Acts 24:12). And, in particular, who would dare suggest that good people of other faiths who have truly sought God and endeavoured to live Godly lives could not be spoken for? And the reverse, who would dare suggest that all people proclaiming themselves as Christians will automatically be spoken up for?

CHAPTER 3

Research: What is a Near Death Experience?

Research into the subject of NDEs has been considerable over the last forty years, with many thousands of cases now in the *Journal of Near-Death Studies* in IANDS' archives.

Very revealing is the commonality of the findings of the various researchers, cross-culturally and cross-nationally, as to what is involved in an NDE—i.e. its components.

CRITICAL RESEARCHERS

1. Dr Raymond Moody

The first of the serious investigators, Dr Raymond Moody, studied hundreds of NDEs and published his results in 1975. He described what, through his investigations, he saw as the "standard" NDE. His work attracted other researchers to the subject, and the formation, three years later, of the International Association of Near-Death Studies. Moody offered the following composite scenario based on his extensive research.[15]

> A man is dying, and as he reaches the point of greatest physical distress he hears himself pronounced dead by his doctor. He begins to hear an uncomfortable noise, a loud ringing or buzzing, and at the same time feels himself moving very rapidly through a long dark tunnel. After this, he suddenly finds himself outside of his own physical body, but still in the immediate physical environment, and he sees his own body from a distance, as though he is a spectator. He watches the resuscitation attempt from this unusual vantage point and is in a state of emotional upheaval.

After a while, he collects himself and becomes more accustomed to his odd position. He notices that he still has a body, but one of a very different nature and with very different powers from the physical body he has left behind.

Soon other things begin to happen. Others come to meet and help him. He glimpses the spirits of relatives and friends who have already died and a loving warm spirit of a kind he has never encountered before, a being of light, appears before him.

This being asks him a question non-verbally, to make him evaluate his life and helps him along by showing him a panoramic, instantaneous playback of the major events of his life [a life review].

At some point he finds himself approaching some sort of a barrier or border apparently representing the limit between earthly life and the next life. Yet, he finds that he must go back to earth, that the time for his death has not yet come. At this point he resists, for by now he is taken up with his experience in the afterlife and does not want to return. He is overwhelmed by intensive feelings of joy, love, and peace. Despite his attitude however he somehow reunites with his physical body and lives.

Later he tries to tell others but he has trouble in doing so. In the first place he can find no human words adequate to describe these unearthly episodes. He also finds that others scoff so he stops telling other people. Still, the experience affects him profoundly, especially his views about death and his relationship to life.

2. IANDS

Following the intense interest in Moody's research, the International Association for Near-Death Studies (IANDS) was founded in 1978. It was incorporated in the state of Connecticut, USA, in 1981 for the purpose of "meeting the needs of early researchers and experiencers"[16] and claiming that it was the first organisation in the world "devoted to the study of near death and similar experiences, and their relationship to human consciousness. Today its varied membership represents every continent but the Antarctic."[17]

IANDS states that the pioneers whose studies brought NDEs to the public's attention in the 1970s, following Moody's research were psychiatrists Elisabeth Kübler-Ross and George Ritchie MD, and in following years, Kenneth Ring PhD, Michael Sabom MD, Bruce Greyson MD, and others. They extended and broadened the early findings and stimulated additional interest in the field.

It is relevant to note that all of these were members of the medical profession, one which has been historically lukewarm in accepting the reality of NDEs.

The IANDS' definition of a near death experience is a summary based upon many submissions to its *Journal of Near-Death Studies*:

> An NDE is a profound psychological event that may occur to a person close to death or, if not near death, in a situation of physical or emotional crisis. Because it includes transcendental and mystical elements, an NDE is a powerful event of consciousness; it is not a mental illness.
>
> Whether happening "truly near death" or under benign circumstances, the NDE contains powerful images and emotions, usually of peace and love though sometimes, terror, despair, guilt. An NDE may include an out-of-body-experience and vivid perceptions of movement, light, darkness; encounters with deceased love ones, unfamiliar entities and/or spiritual presences; sometimes a life review, a landscape, a sense of overpowering knowledge and purpose. The after-effects of an NDE or related experience are enduring, often powerful, and may be life altering.

IANDS' comprehensive research reveals that an NDE may begin with an out-of-body experience, a very clear perception of being somehow separate from one's physical body, possibly even hovering nearby and watching events going on around the body. It typically includes a sense of moving often at great speed and usually through a dark space into a fantastic landscape and encountering beings that may be perceived as sacred figures, deceased family members or friends, or unknown entities. A pinpoint of indescribable light may grow to surround the person in brilliant but not painful radiance; unlike physical light, it is not merely visual but is sensed as being an all-loving presence.

Many NDE accounts include only one or two of the common

features which IANDS identifies as "intensity, peace, love, bliss, ineffability of experience, life changing effects" but those were so powerful that its details will be clearly remembered for decades, unlike a dream.

3. Dr Peter Fenwick

In England at the time of his research, Dr Peter Fenwick was a consultant neurophysiologist at St. Thomas' Hospital and a consultant neuropsychiatrist at the Maudsley Hospital, and President of the British branch of IANDS. He has an impressive track record for his empirical research into consciousness. In recent years he has searched for scientific corroboration of near death experiences. He studied 345 patients who had suffered cardiac arrest for evidence of NDEs. This is his description:

> A near death experience is a distinct subjective experience that people sometimes report after a near death episode. In a near death episode, a person is either clinically dead, near death, or in a situation where death is likely or expected. These circumstances include serious illness or injury, such as from a car accident, military combat, childbirth, or suicide attempt.
>
> People in profound grief, in deep meditation, or just going about their normal lives have also described experiences that seem just like NDEs, even though these people were not near death. Many NDErs have said the term "near death" is not correct; they are sure that they were in death, not just near death .
>
> Near death experiencers (NDErs) have reported two types of experiences, but most NDErs have reported pleasurable NDEs. These experiences involve mostly feelings of love, joy, peace, and/or bliss. A small number of NDErs have reported distressing NDEs. These experiences involve mostly feelings of terror, horror, anger, isolation, and/or guilt. Both types of NDErs usually report that the experience was hyper-real—even more real than earthly life.

All researchers draw the distinction Fenwick makes when he points out that people report NDEs after a "near-death episode". They also agree that similar reports sometimes come from people who have not had a near death episode.

In the study by Fenwick of 345 patients who had suffered cardiac arrest sixty-two of these (forty-nine men and thirteen women) reported an NDE. Of these, thirty-five recalled a full-blown NDE:

> In our findings 62 patients (18%) reported an NDE, of whom 41 (12%) described a core experience. Occurrence of the experience was not associated with duration of cardiac arrest or unconsciousness, medication, or fear of death before cardiac arrest. Frequency of NDE was affected by how we defined NDE, the prospective nature of the research in older cardiac patients, age, surviving cardiac arrest in first myocardial infarction, more than one cardiopulmonary resuscitation (CPR) during stay in hospital, previous NDE, and memory problems after prolonged CPR. Depth of the experience was affected by sex, surviving CPR outside hospital, and fear before cardiac arrest. Significantly more patients who had an NDE, especially a deep experience, died within 30 days of CPR.
>
> A feeling of calmness and peace, watching resuscitation attempts from above, entering a tunnel, meeting a Being of Light, seeing dead relatives and friends, and reluctantly agreeing to return.

4. Dr Pim van Lommel

Near death experiences in survivors of cardiac arrest have been an ongoing study in the Netherlands by Pim van Lommel and his associates Ruud van Wees, Vincent Meyers and Ingrid Elfferich.[18] His aim has been to establish the cause of the NDEs and assess factors that affect their frequency, depth, and content. His study focuses on NDEs that people report after life-threatening experiences. A key finding is that modern techniques of resuscitation have increased the frequency of NDEs. His study shows that these experiences are similar in content and effect despite cultural differences—it is rather the language used to make sense of these experiences which distinguishes them according to individual, cultural and religious factors.

Van Lommel's study shows that NDEs are reported in a variety of circumstances, including:

- cardiac arrest in myocardial infarction (clinical death)

- shock in postpartum loss of blood or in preoperative complications
- septic or anaphylactic shock
- electrocution
- coma resulting from traumatic brain damage
- intracerebral hemorrhage or cerebral infarction
- attempted suicide
- near drowning
- asphyxia
- apnoea.

Deathbed visions are a similar phenomenon identified by Van Lommel, usually occurring in the terminal phase of illness or in the aftermath of situations in which death seems imminent, "e.g. serious traffic accidents, mountaineering accidents, or isolation such as with shipwreck".

Van Lommel mentions theories that attempt to account for the NDE phenomenon. One is that physiological changes in the brain, such as brain cells dying due to lack of oxygen, are responsible. Another is that NDEs are a psychological reaction to approaching death. NDEs "could also be linked to a changing state of consciousness (transcendence), in which perception, cognitive functioning, emotion, and sense of identity function independently from normal body-linked waking consciousness".

According to Pim van Lommel, people who report NDEs are sane, and "do not differ from controls with respect to age, sex, ethnic origin, religion, or degree of religious belief".

Some medical researchers, according to van Lommel, say that NDEs happen when the brain is neither conscious nor alive, but van Lommel, in his study of 344 cardiac arrest patients, says patients repeatedly report keen awareness from moments in time when their brains were actually clinically dead.

The explanation, van Lommel says, is that consciousness exists apart from the body, and humans encounter this greater consciousness more fully when earthly life ends.

"People who have had near death experiences say death is just the end of our physical aspects, but it's not the end of who we are," says van Lommel in his book *Consciousness Beyond Life: The Science of Near-Death Experience*. "That is what has been told . . . in religious traditions. They all have the same message: the essence of who we are is immortal."

Another positive statement, indeed, about the reality of the afterlife, as we have just been reviewing in the previous chapter.

Van Lommel listed components of NDEs, and their frequency, revealed by his research:

1. *Awareness of being dead: (50%)*
2. *Positive emotions: (56%)*
3. *Out-of-body experience: (24%)*
4. *Moving through a tunnel: (31%)*
5. *Communication with light: (23%)*
6. *Observation of colours: (23%)*
7. *Observation of a celestial landscape: (29%)*
8. *Meeting with deceased persons: (32%)*
9. *Life review: (13%)*
10. *Presence of border or barrier: (8%)*

5. David San Filippo PhD

David San Filippo is a licensed mental health counsellor practising in Florida, USA. He is a certified disability management specialist, and a certified cognitive behavioural specialist who has been working in human services more than twenty-five years. His counselling and consulting service specialises in helping adults overcome issues related to personal development, trauma, grief and NDEs.

His website contains a library section, which is an excellent resource for general research in human science in the areas of philosophy, psychology, sociology and theology. He summarises an NDE as follows:

1. *A sense of being dead.*
2. *A sense of peace and painlessness.*
3. *A sense of separation from the physical body.*
4. *The sense of passing through a tunnel.*
5. *A sense of an encounter with recognisable ethereal entities, such*

as family, friends, angels or religious personages. These spirits may appear to be enveloped in light.

6. *A sense of rising rapidly into the heavens.*
7. *A sense of an encounter with a Being of Light, which emanates unconditional love. This being has been described as God or Allah.*
8. *An experience of a panoramic, total life review and sense of self judgement about one's life while bathed in the unconditional love of the Being of Light.*
9. *A sense of reluctance to return to the world of the living.*
10. *A sense of a compression or absence of time and sensing no restrictions of space but a freedom to go where the experiencer chooses.*

6. Craig Mitchell

Australian researcher, Craig Mitchell, is an ambulance rescue officer in New South Wales who has brought several people back to life, including the late Kerry Packer, who famously declared that he had been to the other side and there was nothing there, a statement which will be examined later, because it goes to the heart of the reality of NDEs.

Mitchell has gathered stories from all over Australia[19] about what is really on the other side, if anything, and what it means. He has also explored those whose lives have been completely transformed and the quandary of those who wanted to stay. His book is highly recommended for those who would like to learn more about NDEs.

Mitchell says that just as no two people have identical personalities, so it is that no two people have the same NDE, but a pattern, as follows, has emerged in the descriptions of the many Australian experiencers whom he has researched.

> Time as we know it is non-existent, so it is difficult to say how long a person is in the initial state (OBE) before progressing to the next stage, or where and when the afterlife is encountered.
>
> They hear a noise, similar to a ringing or a buzzing sound, which gradually becomes louder.[20] Once they have left their body they find themselves floating above their physical body only to see resuscitation

attempts being made. Having reached this stage some people describe travelling down a long tunnel with great speed; others, walking through a mist that gradually disperses to reveal a rolling landscape of unsurpassed beauty that compares to nothing that we know of on this wonderful planet.

Now they see a light, dim at first, then clear and vibrant and beckoning. They sense that within this light, there is a being that appears to be the light itself. Here they have a meeting with dead friends or relatives and talk with them in what most describe as a telepathic conversation.

The feeling that people experience at this place is one of peace and tranquillity and of utmost warmth and love. However many people have difficulty in describing the feeling using mere language, claiming that the words cannot even start to describe the experience of their feelings.

The "Being of Light" asks a question that makes the person evaluate their life. Then follows an instantaneous life review, often described as being like a slide show or a movie. This is not judgmental but takes the person back through the major events of their life.

At some point in the experience, the person finds themselves approaching a barrier or long wide hedge but they do not cross this as they are told to return. They are usually counselled by a voice saying: "It's not your time yet" or letting the person know that they have to return for someone else's welfare.

After the event the NDEr describes overwhelmingly positive feelings —of being ecstatic at the wonder and beauty of what they experienced, thrilled at the privilege of having experienced what they describe as a miracle, grateful that something so incredible could have happened to them, in awe of the experience, humbled by the magnitude of the event. Yet they usually find it hard to tell loved ones and friends of the experience, for fear of being ridiculed and because of the inadequacy of language.

If any one point stands out in Mitchell's account, and those of other researchers, it is what he describes as the "Being of Light" and the varying identifications, if any, given it. So profound and powerful is that theme of light that it will be the subject of a later chapter in this work.

7. Jeffrey Long

Dr Long is a man of science, specifically a radiation oncologist in Houma, Louisiana, who established the non-profit Near Death Experience Research Foundation (NDERF), and has served on the board of IANDS. NDERF published results of a survey of 613 near death experiencers. Long points out that no two NDEs are identical, but like other researchers quoted earlier, adds that a pattern of common elements emerges in his research. He summarises as follows:

1. *OBE [out-of-body experience] separation of consciousness from the physical body.*
2. *Heightened senses.*
3. *Intense and generally positive emotions or feelings.*
4. *Passing into or through a tunnel.*
5. *Encountering a mystical or brilliant light.*
6. *Encountering other beings, either mystical beings or deceased relatives or friends.*
7. *A sense of alteration of time or space.*
8. *A life review.*
9. *Encountering unworldly ("heavenly") realms.*
10. *Encountering or learning special knowledge.*
11. *Encountering a boundary or barrier.*
12. *A return to the body, either voluntary or involuntary.*

8. P.M.H. Atwater L.H.D.

Because of three NDEs of her own, and her extensive research into other people's, nobody is better qualified, I suggest, than Atwater, to describe and define, the elements of an NDE. She has been a member of IANDS since its inception, written several journal articles and published three books listed in the bibliography.

Her latest book, *The Complete Idiot's Guide to Near Death Experiences*, written in conjunction with David Morgan, may be light-hearted in style; nevertheless it is apposite to note that she is considered a foremost researcher and an authority on the subject.

Some might be dismissive because of its style, but I rate it as one of the most comprehensive reference books of any that I have studied on the subject of NDEs. Atwater has also given, in an earlier work, *Beyond the Light* published in 1994, a detailed summary of NDE patterns based on her own NDEs in 1977 and her investigation into the findings of other researchers.

Her further credentials are impressive,[21] claiming "three thousand plus interviews with experiencers", of which seven hundred, because of their greatest depth, she offers for her pattern as follows:

- A sensation of floating out of one's body, often followed by an out-of-body-experience (OBE) where all that goes on around the "vacated" body is both seen and heard accurately and in detail.
- Passing through a dark tunnel or black hole, or encountering some kind of darkness. This is usually accompanied by a feeling or sensation of movement or an acceleration. "Wind" may be heard or felt, a swooshing sound may predominate.
- Headed towards and entering into a light at the end of the darkness, a loving light of warmth and brilliance, with the possibility of seeing people, animals, plants, lush outdoors, and even cities within that light.
- Greeted by friendly voices, people, or beings, who may be strangers, loved ones, or perhaps religious figures? Conversation can ensue; information or a message may be given, as part of the scenario.
- Seeing a panoramic view of the life just lived, from birth to death or in reverse order, sometimes becoming a "reliving" rather than a dispassionate viewing. The person's life can be reviewed in its entirety or in segments. This is often accompanied by a feeling or need to assess gains or losses made during the life, so the individual can be aware of what was learned or not learned. Other beings can be involved in the assessment or offer advice. It is possible for such "memories" to be open-ended and to include all existent knowledge, not just personal revelations.
- A different sense of time and space, discovering that time and space do not exist, along with losing the need to recognise such measurements as neither valid nor necessary.
- A reluctance to return to the earth plane, but invariably coming to recognise that either one's job on earth is not finished, or a mission is

yet to be performed, before one can return to stay.
- Disappointment at being revived, feeling a need to shrink or somehow squeeze to fit back into the physical body. There can be unpleasantness, even anger or tears, at the realisation that one is back and no longer on "The Other Side".
- Fear of death either subsided or disappears altogether.

A particularly impressive summary.

9. Tibetan Buddhist, Lingza Chokyi

It is valuable to include a cross-cultural reference in establishing the elements and nature of an NDE. Rcference was made earlier to the Buddhists' belief in reincarnation. However, one will see in what follows that their objective, through their "bardo" experience—which they equate to an NDE—is eventually to escape from the cycle of reincarnation, and move on spiritually to higher realms.

A simple analogy, for reincarnation and escaping from it, can be found in my own embarrassing experience of school, when I was told by the headmaster that I would have to repeat Year Seven before I could be allowed to move upwards—that is, that I was not yet qualified to proceed to the next higher level.

What follows about "bardos" is quoted verbatim from an article by Kevin Williams on an NDE website (http://www.near death.com/religion/buddhism/lingza-chokyi.hotmail):

> A curious phenomenon, little known in the West, but familiar to Tibetans, is the delok. In Tibet, delok means returned from death, and traditionally deloks are people who seemingly "die" as a result of an illness, and find themselves traveling in the bardo—one of many Tibetan Buddhist afterlife states. They visit the hell realms, where they witness the judgment of the dead and the suffering of hell, and sometimes they go to paradises and Buddha realms. They can be accompanied by a deity, who protects them and explains what is happening.
>
> After a week the delok is sent back to the body with a message from the "Lord of Death" for the living, urging them toward spiritual practice and a beneficial way of life. Often the deloks have great difficulty making people believe their story, and they spend the rest of their lives

recounting their experiences to others in order to draw them toward the path of wisdom.

The biographies of some of the more famous deloks, such as Dawa Drolma, who was one of the great Lamas of the century, tell us that at the age of 16 she fell ill and died, but returned to her body after five days. For the benefit of others she recorded every detail of her experiences in the bardo and pure realms. The experiences of deloks were often sung all over Tibet by traveling minstrels. A number of aspects of the delok correspond not only with, as you would expect, the bardo teachings, such as the "Tibetan Book of the Dead", but also with the near death experience.

THE KEY ISSUE

Comparing the components and patterns put forward by the researchers from the USA, Britain, the Netherlands, Australia, and Asia, with those of IANDS—which has collated all these findings in its *Journal of Near-Death Studies*—has been a lengthy but necessary exercise in order to demonstrate that considerable commonality has been shown.

All refer to the out-of-body-experience, the tunnel, the light, the perceiving of deceased relatives or friends. All make reference in some form or another to intense emotion in the form of peace, bliss, or joy, even though in some cases subjects initially find themselves in some sort of a hellish place, from which they are released and progress to a more blissful state.

One finds strong similarities between each of their definitions, but it is important to notice, as will be shown when reviewing individual cases, that not every NDE necessarily embraces all of these elements. Of all the intensive investigators however Atwater's summary stands out because of the volume of cases investigated and her own personal experiences.

This commonality, from independent researchers in different parts of the world covering many thousands of NDEs, proves nothing but it is a powerful argument for the truth of the experiences, and against the sceptics who see NDEs as delusional, drug induced, a dream, or hallucinatory.

But the question may be asked whether the NDE is some new "fad", as some saw it, as spiritualism was in the late 19th and early 20th centuries. In what follows, I look at evidence that it is not a new phenomenon but has been known of as far back in history as the time of Plato, long before the time of Christ.

CHAPTER 4

Historical

Although IANDS as an organisation dates back only to the 1970s, there is nothing new about NDEs per se; the 1970s were the years when they were given a name, which led to the establishment of IANDS, and launched collaborative study internationally. However, history throws up many examples of the phenomenon prior to those formative years.

1. Plato (429–347 B.C.)

We can go back as far Plato, who recounts in *The Republic* the resuscitation of the man Er. Er dies in battle, but revives on his funeral pyre and tells of his journey in the afterlife, including an account of reincarnation and celestial spheres.[22]

> With many other souls as his companions, Er had come across an awesome place with four openings—two into and out of the sky and two into and out of the earth. Judges sat between these openings and ordered the souls which path to follow: the good were guided into the path in the sky, the immoral were directed below. But when Er approached the judges he was told to remain, listening and observing in order to report his experience to mankind.
>
> After seven days in the meadow the souls and Er were required to travel further. After four days they reached a place where they could see a rainbow shaft of light brighter than any they had seen before. After another day's travel they reached it. This was the spindle of Necessity. Several women, including Lady Necessity, her daughter and the Sirens were present. The souls were then organized into rows and were each given a lottery token apart from Er.
>
> Then of their lottery tokens, they were required to come forward in

order and choose their next life. Er recalled the first to choose a new life, a man who had not known the terrors of the underground, but had been rewarded in the sky, hastily chose a powerful dictatorship. Upon further inspection he realised that, among other atrocities, he was destined to eat his own children. Er observed that this was often the case of those who had been through the path in the sky, whereas those who had been punished often chose a better life. Many preferred a life different from their previous experience. Animals chose human lives while humans often chose the apparently easier lives of animals.

As they lay down at night to sleep each soul was lifted up into the night in various directions for rebirth, completing their journey. Er remembered nothing of the journey back to his body. He opened his eyes to find himself lying on the funeral pyre, early in the morning, and able to recall his journey through the afterlife.

2. Venerable Bede (A.D. 672–735)—Benedictine Monk

Bede, known as "the father of English history", wrote of "a certain man" who suddenly came to life again the morning after dying during the night.[23]

I heard other voices mocking and laughing. These voices came nearer and nearer to me, and grew louder and louder. Then I saw that those who were laughing and rejoicing were devils. These devils were dragging along with them souls of men which were howling and lamenting. Amongst them I saw a man and a woman. The devils dragged these souls down into the pit, I could not hear their voices so well.

After a while, some of these dark spirits came up again from the flaming pit. They ran forward and came round me. I was terribly frightened by their flaming eyes, and the stinking fire which came out of their mouths and nostrils. They seemed as if they would lay hold of me with burning tongs, which they held in their hands. I looked around me for help.

Just then I saw something like a star shining in the darkness. The light came from him who had brought me into this place. When he came near, the devils went away.

Then he said: "That fiery, stinking pit which you saw is the mouth of hell, and whosoever goes into it shall never come out again. Go back to your body and live among men again. Examine your actions well, and speak and behave so that you may be with the blessed in heaven." When he had said this, of a sudden, I found myself alive again amongst men.

3. Dante Alighieri (c.1265–c.1321)—Italian Poet

In the 13th century Dante Alighieri wrote a beautiful poem concerning his visit to heaven, part of which appears as the epitaph:

The glory of Him who sets all things in motion
Cleaves through the universe, and it flames again
In different places with a different force.
I have been to that heaven where His light
Beams brightest and seen things that none, returning,
Has the knowledge or the power to repeat,
Because, as it draws near to its desire,
Our intellect sinks down to such a depth
That memory cannot trace its way back there.
Nevertheless, whatever I could treasure
Up in my mind about that sacred kingdom
Shall now become the subject of my song.

4. Mother Julian of Norwich (c.1342–c.1416)

Mother Julian was an "anchoress", a religious recluse, who had a series of deathbed visions of Jesus Christ, which she wrote about in her literary work *Revelations of Divine Love*. It is important to note here that they were "near to death" experiences, rather than the classic "return from death" experience described by Bede et al.

Very little is known about Julian's life. Even her name is unknown; the name Julian simply derives from the fact that her anchoress's cell was built onto the wall of the Church of St. Julian in Norwich. Her writings indicate that she was probably born around 1342 and died around 1416. She may have been from a privileged family that lived in Norwich, or nearby. Norwich was at the time the second largest city in England.

Plague epidemics were rampant during the 14th century and, according to some scholars, Julian may have become an anchoress whilst still unmarried, or, as a widow, who had lost her family in the plague. Becoming an anchoress may have served as a way to quarantine her from the rest of the population. There is scholarly debate as to whether Julian was a nun in a nearby convent or even a laywoman.

When she was thirty and living at home, Julian suffered from a severe illness. Whilst apparently on her deathbed, she had a series of intense visions of Jesus Christ, which ended by the time she recovered from her illness on 13 May 1373. In *Revelations of Divine Love*, believed to be the earliest surviving book in English by a woman, Julian wrote immediately after they had happened about fifteen visions in total, focussing upon the nature of God as love, which she had experienced in those visions.[24]

5. Ernest Hemingway (1899–1961)

What happened to the famous novelist Ernest Hemingway, as recounted by Atwater,[25] changed his life, and is an example of the typical brief or initial near death experience. During World War I, Hemingway was wounded by shrapnel while fighting on the banks of the Piave River, near Fossalta, Italy. He convalesced in Milan. In a letter from there to his family, he made this cryptic statement:

> Dying is a very simple thing. I've looked at death and really I know.

Years later, Hemingway explained to a friend what had occurred on that fateful night in 1918:

> A big Austrian trench mortar bomb, of the type that used to be called ash cans, exploded in the darkness. I died then. I felt my soul or something coming right out of my body, like you'd pull a silk handkerchief out of a pocket by one corner. It flew around and then came back and went in again and I wasn't dead anymore.

6. Carl Jung (1875–1961)—Psychiatrist

In more modern times, in 1944, in a hospital in Switzerland, the world-renowned psychiatrist Carl G. Jung, had a heart attack and then a near death experience. His vivid encounter with the Light, plus the intensely meaningful insights, led Jung to conclude that his experience came from something real and eternal.

> It seemed to me that I was high up in space. Far below I saw the globe of the Earth, bathed in a gloriously blue light. I saw the deep blue sea and the continents. Far below my feet lay Ceylon, and in the distance ahead of me the subcontinent of India. My field of vision did not include the whole Earth, but its global shape was plainly distinguishable and its outlines shone with a silvery gleam through that wonderful blue light.
>
> After contemplating it for a while, I turned around. I had been standing with my back to the Indian Ocean, as it were, and my face to the north. Then it seemed to me that I made a turn to the south. Something new entered my field of vision. A short distance away I saw in space a tremendous dark block of stone, like a meteorite. It was about the size of my house, or even bigger. It was floating in space, and I myself was floating in space.
>
> As I approached the steps leading up to the entrance into the rock, a strange thing happened: I had the feeling that everything was being sloughed away; everything I aimed at or wished for or thought, the whole phantasmagoria of earthly existence, fell away or was stripped from me—an extremely painful process.
>
> This experience gave me a feeling of extreme poverty, but at the same time of great fullness. Everything seemed to be past; what remained was a "fait accompli", without any reference back to what had been. There was no longer any regret that something had dropped away or been taken away. On the contrary: I had everything that I was, and that was everything.
>
> Something else engaged my attention as I approached the temple. I had the certainty that I was about to enter an illuminated room and would meet there all those people to whom I belong in reality. There I would at last understand—this too was a certainty—what historical nexus I or my life fitted into.
>
> While I was thinking over these matters, something happened that caught my attention. From below, from the direction of Europe, an image floated up. It was my doctor, or rather, his likeness framed by a

> golden chain or a golden laurel wreath. As he stood before me, a mute exchange of thought took place between us. The doctor had been delegated by the Earth to deliver a message to me, to tell me that there was a protest against my going away. I had no right to leave the Earth and must return. The moment I heard that, the vision ceased.
>
> I was profoundly disappointed, for now it all seemed to have been for nothing. The painful process of defoliation had been in vain, and I was not to be allowed to enter the temple, to join the people in whose company I belonged.

Jung said it was three weeks before he made up his mind to return to this world which he saw as artificial and therefore doubted his ability to see that it was important. He resented the fact that his doctor had brought him back to "life", and became angry with him for doing so, such was the wonder of his experience. This is one of his memorable statements:

> The unconscious psyche believes in life after death.

CHAPTER 5

Case Studies

"I don't know. Somehow it's not the way I pictured it"

1. Ian Cochrane: "Return from Death" Experience

The first of the case studies is a person I can vouch for personally in terms of integrity. It is an example of what I deem the "classic" near death experience, in which the experiencer returns to life after being considered clinically dead.

This case was a catalyst, following my limited experience as a child, in my undertaking a study of NDEs. I knew the experiencer well, knew him as a person of integrity, sober minded, not given to fanciful inventions, so I asked him if he would put his NDE in writing for me. His letter to me follows:

Lisarow NSW
03.04.1990
Dear John;
You are not forgotten. In response to your request my experience, perhaps the best of my life, was thus: having a history of atrial fibrillation with some episodes of a life threatening nature, five ambulance trips to cardiac wards and five "restarts" to shock the heart back into rhythm a specialist decided upon a form of examination of the heart which involves the introduction of silver-tipped probes on fibre-glass rods, three along a major vein in the thigh and one along a vein from the elbow.

These are gently eased along the veins into the heart where the locations are monitored on a TV screen and monitor. Patient is conscious but relaxed with Valium. Electrical currents are introduced selectively and heart responds with thumps, bumps, brief sprints, momentary stops and all the variety of disrhythmia to which one has become accustomed.

The room was crowded; I assume we had experts and learners. You are asked questions constantly and respond trying all the while to remain calm! They made an error, I went into ventricular fibrillation where the major chamber of the heart rushes off at hundreds of beats per minute. My jaw rattled, my throat muscles tensed. I thought, "look out, this is bad news!"—then grey out.

In an instant I was twenty or so years old, lean, lithe and healthy, relaxed, warm, content, young. I was walking across soft warm goldish sand between an open stand of "palm trees". I was conscious of the softest of soft tropic air movement. My shorts were lightweight, laundered, thin, loose. I slid a greenish super-lightweight tropic style shirt off my shoulders. It slid down one side of my back with a sensual whisper of touch.

I knew I was going "there", walking toward the "sun", which drew me toward it with its inviting glow and warmth, the most delightful yellowish colour imaginable across the clean clear blue green water.

Was I to walk on the water? I don't know. One step short of the water I thumped back into the theatre. A ring of anxious faces perspiring—and grey. Everything was grey, I was old, I hurt, and I did not like being pulled back. "My God, I thought we lost you," said one doctor; "we did," said another.

Later I opened and read their report to my G.P. "Heart stopped 2.4 minutes. Five attempts to restart using increasing amounts of D.C. current, expressed in percentages. Abnormality expected not detected."

Trust this is of some value to your research. It is of immense value to me. I know we need not fear death but can look forward to it! I am able to tell people close to death "welcome it, it's going to be the best experience ever!" I can now tell those grieving the death of another. . . "Rejoice".

Best regards: Ian Cochrane.

Rejoice indeed!

2. Howard Storm: Professor, Atheist and Sceptic, Becomes a Christian Minister Following his NDE

Prof. Storm's NDE warrants investigation in some detail, for not only does it include most of the components of NDEs as identified by researchers and arguments for and against their reality, but also, most importantly, finds him initially in a place which we would certainly describe as "hell", before his escape from that place, the essence of which he said is "loveless".

What follows is taken from his autobiography published in 2005.[26]

In June 1985, Storm was leading a group of students on an art tour of France, accompanied by his wife. On the last day of the tour, without warning, he fell to the ground screaming with intense pain, and was rushed to hospital by ambulance. Shortly after arriving he was told that an operation was essential as he had a hole in his duodenum; however, his pain was so intense that he not only believed that he was going to die, but was ready to do so.

Storm had been brought up a Protestant, but by the time he went to university had lost all faith, and became more than an agnostic; he was now a confirmed atheist, who felt nothing but despair and hopelessness at the thought of dying.

Soon he became unconscious, but eventually opened his eyes to find himself staring at his body lying on the bed. He found this out-of-body experience extremely agitating and he started shouting at his wife as she sat beside the bed. She however, took no notice nor gave any evidence of hearing him.

At this point Storm felt voices—seemingly friendly—calling him by name from outside the room. He could see vague figures but they wouldn't come close enough for him to see them clearly. Although he asked them specific questions, they would only give vague answers and were insisting that he should accompany them. Reluctantly, he complied, going on a long journey where there was no landscape or architecture, only an ever thickening, darkening haze.

Finally, Storm said that he would go no further, at which his captors started kicking and punching him, and the more he screamed and struggled the better they liked it. Eventually, unable to fight any further, he fell to the ground and his tormentors seemed to lose interest in him. The similarity of this experience to Bede's description in the previous chapter is remarkable.

At this point, a "voice said to my mind," as he describes it, "pray to God." He began to argue that he didn't believe in God, and anyway he didn't know how to pray. Three times the voice insisted, and he tried to remember long forgotten words such as "God Bless America" and "The Lord is my Shepherd." Soon his thoughts became mutterings and the attackers started screaming at him that there was no God, but he continued shouting little pieces of the 23rd Psalm and the Lord's Prayer, even though he was not convinced of the truth of them. Nevertheless, the creatures retreated as if he had thrown boiling water at them. Now he was alone in a state of utter hopelessness: he didn't know what to do, and didn't want to exist any more.

It was in this feeling of deepest despair that a tune from his childhood, his Sunday School days, started going through his head. This was "Jesus Loves me this I Know" and he desperately wanted it to be true, so with every ounce of his being he screamed into the darkness "Please, Jesus, save me." He meant it and wanted it with every fibre of his being.

As he did so a faint star appeared in the darkness, growing rapidly until soon it was an indescribably brilliant light becoming brighter and brighter. Slowly, all his wounds disappeared, he became whole and well, and he described the light as good, and something of indescribable beauty.

It was his "road to Damascus" conversion. One minute he was an atheist, and the next every part of him wanted Jesus. He said he had lost every ounce of his pride, his egotism, his self dependence, and his reliance on his much self-exalted intellect. All the things which he had lived his life for, had made his god, had let him down; now he wanted only the hope that had been planted in him as a small child, but had abandoned. He knew that the light knew him better than anyone knew him, and that he was loved in a way that he had never been loved before.

He called this light the "Angel of Light", who was surrounded by other lights who were angels, and came and went at his bidding, and were patient, good teachers, who made him feel loved and accepted.

Then he found himself faced with a life review in which the angels wanted to show him details of his life, which he was opposed to, because of shame at the life he had led, and his denial of God. But in that review it was the people with whom he had interacted which the angels concentrated on, rather than events which mattered. He saw himself constantly withdrawing from people and living in his own selfish world, becoming increasingly unhappy although he was successful, getting promotions at work, making good money, and being seen as a "wonderful guy".

The angels showed him how he had turned away from the Lord, how God had tried to reach him in so many different ways, tried to reach him through good people loving him and trying to open up his heart.

Having seen the whole of his life brought in front of him, he told the angels everything had changed for him and that now all that mattered was to go to heaven. But the angels told him that was not possible, because he was not ready and he had to go back and live the life which God had wanted him to. Although Storm argued strongly against this, the angels were adamant, albeit gentle. Heaven was not an option for him yet, he must return, and suddenly he found himself back in his body again.

Storm said that people had asked him many times whether he had dreamed all this, and there were times when he thought he may have. However, the "proof was in the pudding", the experience had changed his life completely. Not only did he become, eventually, a full time minister of the United Church of Christ, but it changed the way he felt.

Where there was once melancholy and cynicism, now there was genuine joy and peace all the time, joy and peace which he tried to spread as best he could. He saw it as important that he encourage people in their faith, and that he be an instrument in leading them to God, which he saw as the work he was sent back to do on earth.

Storm's account of his NDE is of particular interest, in that he is drawn to the light, which is a common feature in other accounts, even though its description varies; it starts as a pinpoint of light, for example, which grows ever larger, whereas Cochrane's was a "sun" drawing him towards "its inviting glow, the most delightful yellowish colour imaginable". Where Storm's account stands out is that he has no hesitation in identifying his experience as a divine encounter, for he declares the "Being of Light" to be Jesus, and claims that he was actually embraced by Him. Although the Being of Light appears in many other NDE accounts, only some of them identify him as Jesus.

3. Patient of Dr Raymond Moody

Her own words about her cardiac arrest:

> I found myself floating up towards the ceiling. I could see everybody around the bed very plainly, even my own body. I thought how odd it was that they were upset about my body. I was fine and wanted them to know that, but there seemed to be no way to let them know. It was

as though there were a veil or screen between me and the others in the room.

I became aware of an opening, if I can call it that. It appeared to be elongated and dark, and I began to zoom through it. I was puzzled yet exhilarated. I came out of this tunnel into a realm of soft brilliant love and light. The love was everywhere. It surrounded me and seemed to soak through into my very being.

At some point I was shown, or saw, the events of my life. They were in a kind of vast panorama. All of this is just indescribable. People I knew who had died were there with me in the light, a friend who had died in college, my grandfather, and a great-aunt, among others. They were happy beaming.

I didn't want to go back, but I was told that I had to by a man in the light. I was being told that I had not completed what I had to do in my life.

I came back into my body with a sudden lurch.

4. Medical Practitioner

This is a transcript of a live presentation given by a doctor, an erudite man of science, member of a profession often sceptical about the reality of NDEs—at the 2013 annual IANDS convention, where he talks about his experience. It also may be seen and listened to on YouTube.[27]

It is particularly valuable, because, as I have mentioned before, live presentations are given by people attending the annual convention from many different countries around the world at their own expense, with nothing to gain other than the opportunity to speak of their experience to a sympathetic audience, without fear of being patronised, or ridiculed.

This account is also valuable for the number of elements that have been highlighted previously in NDEs, mentioned in chapter 3. Like Howard Storm, initially he finds himself in a "hellish" state, from which he is rescued.

In 2008, I was a practicing cardiac anesthesiologist. I was Chief of Anesthesiology at a heart hospital and derived my identity and happiness from the work I did and my family. But in August of that year—everything was turned upside down when I was diagnosed with prostate cancer. A routine surgery to treat it, in the same month, led to complications that left me incontinent and in excruciating pain due to scar formation. Due to these complications, I was forced back into surgery a further three times between Aug and Dec 2008.

As if cancer wasn't enough, I was now living in excruciating pain, impotent, incontinent, and wearing diapers. As an anesthesiologist I was the first to advocate the prescription of traditional pain medications to manage the severity of the pain I lived with. I soon learned, however, that the body's quick dependency on the pain medication created the condition of addiction to pain medications within me. I was now a cancer survivor living with post-surgical complications, chronic pain, and addiction. Within a year, I was diagnosed with depression too.

This anaesthetist was back in surgery in December 2010 for insertion of an artificial urinary sphincter. After surgery he was very sick, running a high fever up to 105°F. His entire pelvic area including the penis and scrotum was red and badly swollen. Despite being treated with heavy duty antibiotics, he was making no improvement and he realised something was very very wrong.

On Christmas Eve he was admitted as an emergency sepsis patient. On Christmas Day it was decided that emergency surgery was necessary to drain out pus from the pelvic region and to remove the foreign body, the artificial sphincter.

The last memory he has of these preparations is of a catheter being inserted to drain his bladder. The pain was searing, so intense that his next memory is of no longer being in his body. In his own words he had "disassociated my awareness from the location of the body itself, and yet I was fully aware and present outside of my body, I was in what I can only describe as a different plane of existence." He was aware that "a consciousness that was ME, but was not limited to the location of my body was completely intact that night and during surgery, and not only was it completely intact, but it was more acute and expanded"; so much so that he can remember looking down at his body from 10 to 15 feet above. He remembers the awful smell of the puss, the nurses scenting the surgical masks with eucalyptus water, and the anaesthetist making a coarse joke.

He then had a "hellish" experience, similar to Howard Storm's, finding himself in a place where a great wild fire was burning and where dark entities were rushing about, where he could hear other souls screaming and suffering, and where he was badly tortured. What had he done to deserve this? he wondered. Was it perhaps punishment for behaviour in past lives? As he experienced this horror he began to have a strong awareness that the life he had lived was very materialistic, always about himself, and when he met someone he was always asking what could he get from that person.

The awareness grew on him in this hellish state that he had been living a life without love, that he was not practising forgiveness or compassion towards others—nor indeed himself—and that he had been particularly hard on people whom he considered lower in social status or in the professional hierarchy. He found that he felt deeply sorry for his lack of kindness, and began wishing he could do things differently because he had been behaving with a lack of love to those less fortunate than he was, and misusing his material wealth and social status. He knew then that if he lived again he would have to break those patterns completely and live differently.

But the moment these realisations became crystal clear hell began to fade away. With that his father, who had died twenty years earlier, appeared with his grandfather, took his hand and guided him towards a tunnel at the end of which a white light was glowing. As he moved through the tunnel it was if time and space disappeared. He was in a state of pure harmony—what he describes as *"total, utter, undisturbed bliss which unified all things and beings in the universe"*—this he presumed to be heaven. He found that words are inadequate to describe it. He found himself in the presence of a loving formless light which he understood, or felt, to be the personification of supreme love, knowledge and intelligence.

Here in the midst of profound calmness, light and joy he was greeted by two beings who seemed like young men, who radiated energy and light, and were full of vigour, enthusiasm and love. They informed him that they were his guardian angels and that their names were Michael and Raphael. He had once attended an "angel therapy" session and been told that we all have guardian angels. He had been quite sceptical about that, and now he knew differently.

These angels who communicated without speech then guided him through the beautiful place in which he found himself, amongst fields with many different coloured roses, mountains, a fresh stream flowing with crystal water and cool, soothing air moving gently around, an air of soft and sweet fragrance. From a distance a soft chant was clearly audible.

His helpers taught him that the highest level of consciousness has no form, but an all pervading force, a powerful energy of "PURE LOVE" (sic), and that this is the base reality—the underlying fabric of absolutely everything in the universe—the source of all creation. It was hard for him to describe how he felt in the presence of the light being, pure love pervading everything, all powerful.

He was told that his path from then was to be that of a healer, and that he would have to leave anaesthesiology and materialism behind: *"Now it is time to be healer of the soul, especially the diseases of the soul, of the energy body, of addiction, depression, chronic pain and cancer"*. He was told that the reason he had had to experience the diseases which had befallen him was so as he would have empathy for others, how it felt to be in their shoes. And he was given glimpses of his future which was "writing great books to help others, speaking to large audiences, and helping lots of people".

This was a complete revelation to him as he had always been an anaesthetist who barely spoke to patients—and preferred it that way! Left to himself he would have been happy to continue as an anaesthetist. It was his passion, he was very good at it, he didn't have to interact with people much, and it was providing him with a lifestyle that he had come to enjoy and identify with. But now he could see that he had not been a compassionate man even though he had been very well off. He had revelled in material comfort, loving his work so much that had it been up to him he "would never in a million years" have considered giving it up.

However, here he was being given direct orders from the supremely loving, intelligent, and gentle "Light Being" that his life had to change, that he was being given it back only to live it differently. Nevertheless he felt no resistance because he was in a place of pure love and reassurance. He accepted what he was being shown with silent and profound love, and the awareness that he was being given his life back for the specific purpose of writing and speaking in order to help others battling chronic pain, depression, and addiction.

He next remembers waking up in the hospital's recovery room. Much to the amazement of the medical staff the rate of his healing in the days that followed was almost miraculously quick. He was discharged within 72 hours, the inflammation and pain in his pelvic region decreased astonishingly, and within a few months disappeared altogether.

Life-changing effects due to the reality of his experience

A year later his life was a very different one. The radical changes that followed his near death experience brought life-long ramifications for his family. The family decided to downsize into a much more modest house, he went from driving a Mercedes to a hybrid Toyota, he resigned from anaesthesiology, his medical health was transformed, and he began looking for volunteering opportunities to perform selfless service for others every day. His tendency to addictive behaviour that had led to dependence on pain medications, disappeared completely.

Most profoundly his entire outlook had changed; he was filled with a desire to be of service and to have his voice heard to help people heal. He felt himself still connected to the "Light Being" and recalls with clarity the experience of "Hell" and "Heaven", and of meeting with his father and other family members who had long since died.

Notice how similar his story is to Howard Storm's, a complete transformation in attitude following his near death experience. This goes to the heart of the purpose of this book: to try and determine the "reality" of NDEs, and, if they are real, to consider what further light they may shed on the little we know about the afterlife—which Jesus has confirmed for Christians as enshrined in their creeds, but in which many non-Christians also believe.

Arguably, the life changing effects experienced by many near death experiencers constitute persuasive grounds for accepting the reality of their experiences instead of explaining them away as the effect of imagination, hallucination or some biological cause.

5. NDE Accepted by the *Journal of Near-Death Studies*, 2008

Anonymity observed as requested.

> I was being treated in a hospital for a "chemical imbalance" after the birth of my first child. After having serious marriage problems I stopped sleeping much and was way too "up." About 10 days after the birth I entered the hospital. After an initial assessment they decided I needed to sleep. I was walking down the hall of the hospital with my mom when the nurse approached with the medication. I took the pills and immediately felt the wild symptoms. I knew that I had to find my bed and called out to my mom to take me there. My eyes were rolling up and my tongue felt like it was choking me. I groped to my bed and fell unconscious face down.
>
> I immediately left my body, traveling so fast within this amazing, comforting, all encompassing light (words cannot describe this feeling). I arrived at a place where a being (a guide) held my hand while different parts of my life played out before me like a movie. However everything was from inside of the person I was with at the time. How they felt when I looked at them, talked to them. It was a huge shock. I became full of knowledge that was like a burden to me. I still have to stop myself from telling people about themselves and their behavior today.
>
> Anyway, next came a tunnel. At the end was a group of my family waiting for me in a garden. Far in the distance I could see many things like a beautiful city or large palace. It was strange because it didn't look

like it was on land. Maybe it was an island or something. In between was a small river. It was amazingly beautiful. (Words are not powerful enough to describe these sights). Things smelled wonderful. There was music softly playing but no musicians. Everything was in its natural form. No technology.

My great-grandmother was the strongest presence there—and in life as well, as I knew her until I was 14—and she broke into my amazed reverence and said point blank, "You cannot stay here". I argued. I pleaded. She forced me to look down and all of a sudden I was in the hospital watching the doctor from a height of about 15–20 ft or so. The ceilings were only average height so I was looking through the floor! My mom was on the side of the bed near the door and the nurse was on the other side. The doctor was right on the bed on top of me giving me a needle (adrenaline) into my neck. He was shouting at me "Don't forget to breathe." My mother was crying hard and holding onto the wall for support.

I heard a voice in my head "You have a choice. Will you leave your mother and your baby behind?" The very next moment I took a breath and opened my eyes, smiled at the doctor and said, "What are you so worried about? I am fine", and then I sat up. He freaked out. He pushed me back down and shouted at me to lie still. I tried to reassure him. I told him I saw what he did and that I went someplace wonderful. All he said was, "I'm so glad you came back."

6. Helen's Near Death Experience: Suicide

In an excellent book[28] Jean Ritchie has documented the suicide attempts and subsequent near death experiences of a woman named Helen. Her NDEs demolish the myths accepted by many religious people that suicide and homosexuality are one way tickets to hell.

Although today Helen is very comfortable with the fact that she is a lesbian, coping with it has not always been easy. By the time she was seventeen, she was drinking heavily and experimenting with drugs.

Over the years, her problems greatly escalated which led her to decide to take her own life. After writing suicide notes and taking an overdose of pills and drink, she was rushed to a hospital in very serious condition. Her heart stopped four times, she learned later from the medical staff.

> I remember clearly floating up above myself, and looking down on my body. It was connected to numerous machines. I could see the drip and the oxygen mask. I could see the doctors working to restart my heart with electronic pads. I could see that my parents were there. It felt very peaceful, much better than where I had been before. I was bathed in warmth and light, and the calm was almost tangible. I felt it was up to me to decide where I wanted to be, up there or back in my body, but the peace was so overwhelming that I knew I wanted to stay.
>
> And then I was in a small supermarket, floating between the aisles. It was like any ordinary supermarket, with shelves loaded with goods. My grandmother, who died when I was very young, was at the checkout, and so was my auntie. I knew without anyone telling me that it was my auntie, my mum's sister, although she had died of a brain hemorrhage before I was born. They were beckoning to me to go to them, but through the plate-glass window I could see my parents and my immediate family, also beckoning and urging me to hurry.

The next thing Helen remembers is waking from her coma with the oxygen mask pressing on her face and causing some pain. She felt regret at having left the peace behind.

Helen's second NDE came a couple of years after the first, after another suicide attempt. This time she took pills and tried to swallow bleach. Her partner found her and called an ambulance.

> I was drifting in and out of consciousness, more out than in, but I remember being wheeled from the flat on a stretcher. Again, I floated above and could look down and see two men carrying the stretcher, and I felt secure and safe in the knowledge that I was walking away from all the chaos of my life. Again, I felt it was my decision to walk away.
>
> It was like stepping into a vacuum, there was nothing tangible, no scenery to look at, but a tremendous feeling of being somewhere, like nirvana. I felt okay, as though this was where I was meant to be, as if I had arrived home, and I was at ease with myself for the first time in a long time.

> I also felt at one with the forces of the universe, as though I was part of something much much bigger, and yet I was also the whole of it. It was a tremendously powerful feeling, and such a contrast to the despair and depression that had led me there.

This second time Helen did not see any relatives, and although she experienced the same sense of there being a choice to return to life or continue in that lovely place, she did not feel any panic when she awoke in the hospital a few days later.

> I knew I had not wanted to relinquish the good feelings the place had given me, but at the same time I did not feel regret at returning. This time, the experience seemed to give me strength. I felt refreshed.

She was told by hospital staff that she was lucky to have survived. Helen's two NDEs have taken away any fear she may have had of death, and she now anticipates that when it comes she will once again experience those feelings of peace and tranquility. She does not believe that her experiences encouraged her to make more suicide attempts: suicide, she says, is born of despair with this world, not a hankering after the peace and serenity of the next. Eventually, Helen was able to beat her alcohol and drug addiction. She is back with her partner, studying for a master's degree and doing volunteer work.

7. Two Drownings

In this account, from the archives of the *Journal of Near-Death Studies*, a person who drowned twice in childhood recounts two very different experiences which resulted in different after-effects. The first took place as a toddler and the second as an older child.

> After the moment of my death, I became like a breath, and was "breathed" into the body of a nude, non-gender being. I was very confused and frightened.
>
> At the center of the horizon was a small patch of clouds, a patch which I realized was approaching me. As it approached, I saw that the clouds were actually beings, and as the beings crept closer, I saw that they were lions, seven of them, with enormous wings. When they were close, I viewed them in great detail. Their wingspans were wide enough

that they seemed to envelop the entire horizon. Their paws were enormous, curled under a bit in a relaxed fashion.

Their faces, however, were human, with eyes fierce and kind and loving in a way which I have never experienced on Earth. I felt only comfort now, as if nothing could possibly harm me, and I experienced an overwhelming feeling of complete joy and contentment. This is the moment I was revived. I believe that, had I not been revived, I certainly would have been escorted away with these amazing creatures. I have since always been capable of envisioning this image in great detail, and it is beautiful to me.

I was only a toddler, and when my mother realized I was unconscious, she called a family friend who was a registered nurse who talked my mother through my resuscitation. I received no medical attention afterwards, although I did suffer brain damage. Through my childhood, I experienced petit mal seizures and my short-term memory was permanently damaged.

Her second drowning:

It was summer and my older sister was having a few friends over for her 15th birthday party. We had an in-ground swimming pool with a slide, hemmed in with a privacy fence from the rest of our yard, which was quite large. My sister and her friends were leaving, and as they were shutting the gate, I said, "Hey, watch!" and slid down the slide on my back, head-first. As soon as I hit the water, the girls left, not knowing that I hit my head on the square plug at the bottom of the pool and split my head open. I was not knocked unconscious. I curled into a fetal position, inhaling water. The sun was shining, sparkling through the water, and I saw blood pooling in front of me in contrast with the blue pool. I do not recall feeling any real pain or extreme panic.

I do not have a concept of time, but eventually I could see our house from an aerial view of about 80 feet. I saw the roof of our house, the entire yard, my sister at the gate on the other side of the yard, about 60 feet from the pool fence. I saw my mother mowing the yard around the apple trees, which were quite a distance from the house. I also saw myself, curled up, a tiny figure on the bottom of the pool with blood pooled around my head and neck.

I was then shuttled through a tunnel of rainbow lights at a speed which cannot be described, for a period of time which I cannot estimate. I emerged at the entrance of a beautiful garden, at the center of which was a hall of open pillars, featuring a calm blue sky, with white clouds. There were small plants and rocks surrounding the first few pillars, then the pillars extended into a mist.

I felt a presence to my left, but there was no sound. To my right, a woman was sitting weeping on a stone, being counseled by someone wearing a simple white garment. Though no words were spoken, I heard their conversation intuitively. She was mourning her own death and was very worried about her daughter whom she was leaving when she died. She had died of an incurable illness, however, and couldn't go back, and her counselor was comforting her, communicating that her daughter was grown and would be fine. I could feel this woman's heart breaking.

I was not counseled directly and felt very calm. I knew that I was free to pass down the hall or return to life, that this was my choice, unlike the woman who was unwilling to accept her death. I very much wanted the relief of continuing down the path before me, but I could also envision my body in the pool and by choosing to depart that life, I would be giving up a priceless experience, that no matter how great or small the accomplishments were in this life, or how difficult this life may seem, that the human experience is invaluable and precious, and that everyone's life is this way.

I turned my back to the pillars and awoke in my body before I was found by my sister, opened my eyes briefly, then passed into a deep darkness until my sister found me, pulled me from the pool and resuscitated me. I was potentially dead for about 10 minutes, perhaps longer. The drive to the hospital was about 30 minutes, as we were rural, and I came close to bleeding to death.

The incision on the back of my head was closed with 15 stitches, and I contracted pneumonia. My short-term memory, which was damaged by my previous drowning, did not seem to be affected at all, at least as far as I can tell. My memory problems began from the earlier drowning and did not become worse following the second. I find this rather peculiar.

However, on the way home from my week-long hospital stay, we passed a small house on a country road, very nondescript, yet I immediately knew many things about this house, as if I had lived in it, and was aware of who lived in it. This was the first time I had ever experienced any form of psychic intuition, but I've learned not only to live with it but to abide by it. I do, however, tend to keep it a secret from people.

8. Tibetan Buddhists

Dawa Drolma

At the age of sixteen, Dawa Drolma, now one of the more famous deloks, fell ill and died, but returned to her body after five days. For the benefit of others she recorded every detail of her experiences in the bardo and pure realms.

The experiences of deloks were often sung all over Tibet by travelling minstrels. A number of aspects of the delok correspond not only with, as you would expect, the bardo teachings, such as *The Tibetan Book of the Dead*, but also with the near death experience. Dawa Drolma is the author of the book, *Delok: Journey to Realms Beyond Death*.

Bardos vis-a-vis NDEs

There are many similarities in the various teachings of the afterlife, as revealed in a look at the *Tibetan Book of the Dead* and the NDE. In the NDE, the mind is momentarily released from the body, and goes through a number of experiences, akin to those of the mental body in the "bardo of becoming".

NDEs very often begin with an out-of-body experience: people can see their own body, as well as the environment around them. This coincides with what *The Tibetan Book of the Dead* describes. In the bardo of becoming, the dead are able to see and hear their living relatives, but are unable, sometimes frustratingly, to communicate with them. The mental body in the bardo of becoming is described in *The Tibetan Book of the Dead* as being "like a body of the golden age", and as having almost supernatural mobility and clairvoyance. Near death experiencers also find that the form they have is complete and in the prime of life. They find also that they can travel instantaneously, simply by the power of thought.

In the Tibetan teachings, the mental body in the bardo of becoming meets other beings in the bardo. Similarly, near death experiencers are often able to converse with others who have died.

In the bardo of becoming, as well as many other kinds of visions, the mental body will see visions and signs of different realms. A small percentage of near death experiencers describe visions of inner worlds, paradises, and cities of light with transcendental music. The most astounding similarity is the encounter with the Being of Light, or the "Clear Light" as described in *The Tibetan Book of the Dead.* According to the Tibetan teachings, at the moment of death, the Clear Light dawns in all its splendour before the dying person.

> O son/daughter of an enlightened family . . . your Rigpa is inseparable luminosity and emptiness and dwells as a great expanse of light; beyond birth or death, it is, in fact, the Buddha of Unchanging Light.

Tibetan teachings stress that by recognising yourself as this "clear light", you will attain liberation from the cycle of reincarnation. Many near death experiencers are convinced the Being of Light is their higher self. This is certainly in agreement with the Tibetan teachings.

The life review appears again and again in NDE reports, and demonstrates so clearly the inevitability of karma and the far-reaching and powerful effects of all our actions, words, and thoughts.

The central message near death experiencers bring back from their encounters with death, or the presence of the Being of Light, is exactly the same as that of Buddha and of the bardo teachings: that the essential and most important qualities in life are love and knowledge, compassion and wisdom.

The bardo teachings tell us that life and death are in the mind itself. The confidence which many near death experiencers seem to have after this experience reflects this deeper understanding of mind.

Not all NDE reports, however, are positive, and this corresponds to the Tibetan teachings as well. Some people report experiences of fear, panic, loneliness, desolation, and gloom, all vividly reminiscent of the descriptions of the bardo of becoming.

In many NDE reports, a border or limit is perceived; a point of no return is reached. At this border the experiencer chooses (or is instructed) to return to life, sometimes by the presence of light. Of course in the Tibetan bardo teachings there is no parallel to this, because they describe what happens to a person who actually dies.

It has been said the NDE can be viewed as an evolutionary device to bring about a transformation in humanity as a whole, over a period of years, in millions of persons.[29]

Whether this is true or not depends on all of us: on whether we really have the courage to face the implications of the NDE and the bardo teachings, and by transforming ourselves we transform the future of humanity.

Lingza Chokyi

Lingza Chokyi was a famous delok who lived in the 16th century. In her biography she tells how she failed to realise she was dead, how she found herself out of her body, and saw a pig's corpse lying on her bed, wearing her clothes. Frantically she tried in vain to communicate with her family as they set about the rituals of death. She grew furious with them when they took no notice of her and did not give her a plate of food.

After a while, she heard someone whom she thought was her father calling to her, and she followed him. She arrived in the bardo realm, which appeared to her like a country. From there, she tells us, there was a bridge that led to the hell realms, and to where the Lord of Death was counting the good or evil actions of the dead. In this realm she met various people who recounted their stories, and she saw a great yogin who had come into the hell realms in order to liberate beings.

Finally, Lingza Chokyi was sent back to the world, as there had been an error concerning her name and family, and it was not yet her time to die. With the message from the Lord of Death to the living, she returned to her body and recovered, and spent the rest of her life telling of what she had learned. The phenomenon of the delok was not simply a historical one; it continued up until very recently in Tibet.

9. Another Doctor's NDE

Mary C. Neal MD, is an orthopaedic surgeon. She studied at the University of California Los Angeles School of Medicine, and completed her orthopaedic residency at the University of Southern California. She was the Director of Spine Surgery at the University of Southern California and is a founding partner of Orthopedic Associates of Jackson Hole. Her afterlife experience has been featured on American media including WGN, Dr. Oz, and Fox and Friends. She has served as a church elder, on several non-profit organisation boards, and created the Willie Neal Environmental Awareness Fund. Dr. Neal lives with her family in Jackson Hole, Wyoming.

Her NDE occurred when she was trapped underwater in a kayak—a life changing event that is decribed in her 2012 book *To Heaven and Back*. The following is a transcript of an interview by Amazon.[30]

> Q. *How did you feel when you died? Did you know what was happening?*
>
> A. I was acutely aware of everything that was happening. I knew that my efforts to exit the boat were not working, that I was out of air, and that I was too far from the riverbank for anyone to reach me. I knew that I would probably die. Having grown up with a fear of drowning, I was surprised to find my transition from life to death was seamless, peaceful, and beautiful. I felt quite wonderful.
>
> Q. *What was your faith life like before your death?*
>
> A. Before my near death experience, I believed in God and took my kids to Sunday School but was not particularly religious. Like many accomplished young adults, I felt like I was in control of my life and my future. Although I tried to be a "good" and "moral" person, my faith was not integrated into my daily life and the demands of work and family left little time to think about spirituality.
>
> With my near death experience, the truth of God's promises and the reality of eternal life became a part of my every breath. I am in constant

prayer and regardless of what I am doing, I try to reflect God's love and live for His glory. I try not to miss opportunities to uplift or encourage the spiritual life of others, and I live with gratitude and joy, knowing that I never face challenges alone.

Q. *Why do you think you came back to life?*

A. I certainly didn't want to return to earth, but was given information about some of the work I was yet to complete and wasn't really given a choice. I was expected to share my experiences and my story with others, helping transform their faith into complete trust that God keeps His promises.

Q. *Do you have any regrets about this experience?*

A. I have not a hint of regret. In fact, my death and return to life is the greatest gift I have ever received, and I am continually grateful for having had this experience.

Q. *How do you explain why this happened to you?*

A. I have always been a private person, am not known to be a writer, and do not relish the attention of speaking. I have been asked this question many times. I do not know the answer, but I am a scientist by training, a skeptic by nature, and a very concrete, rational thinker. Perhaps, I was given this job because I have developed a lifetime of credibility.

Q. *How is your experience compared to others who've gone to heaven and come back to physical life?*

A. I have not read many accounts of other people's experiences, but I have had many patients over the years tell me about their own near death experiences. It seems that most stories, mine included, contain some consistent elements—that of an overwhelming sense of God's love and forgiveness, intense peace and beauty and no desire to return to Earth. Everyone recalls the details with precision and each person is profoundly affected by the experience. In these ways, my experience is quite similar.

Q. *What do you want people to know about heaven?*

A. God's unconditional love for each of us is intense, complete, and is reflected in all of Heaven. Before we return to Heaven, our real home, we have an incredible opportunity on Earth to face challenges that will help us learn, grow and to become more Christ-like in the fruits of our spirit. Our time is so short that we need to be about God's business every day.

Other Case Studies Accepted by IANDS Archives

The following selections are taken from accounts submitted to the IANDS archives and thoroughly investigated by IANDS as to their veracity before being accepted.[31] Permission has been given to publish them, but anonymously.

10. Woman in Childbirth

The first account is from a woman who had complications during childbirth over twenty-five years ago. The most striking aspect is an out-of-body experience where she witnessed events that she could not have seen while she was unconscious, including a period when she was clinically dead according to her records. She also recounts some interesting after-effects.

> Apparently whilst giving birth to my son there were complications and I was anesthetized. As I described it to my doctor at the time. I remember just suddenly sort of floating up in the corner of the room and that there was a very bright light. I only remember that I was there, but not in my body! I was looking down at myself and saw the matron literally lifting my ex-husband (slipped her arms under his armpits and heaved him bodily; she was a large woman, my husband was over 6 foot), out of the room. He was asking what's happening, and that he'll just sit in the corner out of the way. The matron said "No, you must leave."
>
> Then I noticed that there was a "stranger" working on me along with my doctor, I didn't know who he was, or where he had come from, or for that matter, when he had entered the room? It seemed to me then and also now that I didn't perceive "time" the way one does normally.
>
> This "stranger" had a bald spot on the crown of his head and wore black, squarish glasses! I do remember wondering who is he? What's he doing? Where did he come from? Is my baby all right? Whilst all this was going through my mind I have to admit that I wasn't scared at all,

just a little confused and also, what I am still a little perplexed about, I was extremely calm and nonplussed by everything that was going on below me. Then I suddenly heard a voice saying it's not my time, I'm needed, and to go back, that everything will be fine. I remember agreeing, wanting to be there for my son.

When I finally "woke up" on the ward, some 2–3 hours later, I started yelling for the matron saying that I wanted to see my son! She finally came in, then she asked me how I knew that I had had a boy? I said that I had seen him whilst she was cleaning him after his birth. She gave me the strangest look and walked out!

Later when my doctor came to see me, I asked him who the "stranger" was that was with him whilst I was "out of it"? He asked how I knew about him, had the matron told me about him, I said no, that I had seen him leaning over the top of me (whilst I was laying on the table/bed). I then described him (as above) and also that he was much shorter than him (my doctor being taller that is). He was quite stunned that I knew so many details about this "stranger" who turned out to be a "specialist" that he (my doctor), had flown in by helicopter (whilst I was "knocked out"), as this happened in a small town and there weren't too many doctors available at this Hospital. I have never met this other doctor either before this all happened nor after.

My doctor believed me, because as he said, how could I have seen the "bald spot" on the "top" of this other doctor's head? He did tell me NOT TO TELL ANYONE OR THEY'D PROBABLY LOCK ME AWAY!! He reiterated that he believed me and found it fascinating but not to speak about it to anyone else!

Apart from this letter, I've only told three people about this occurrence. One was my younger sister . . . she had rung me late one evening, not long after giving birth to her first daughter, my son was about 5 years old at the time. She was most distraught, she had had the same experience during childbirth as I had, as in watching from up in the corner of the room etc., and said she didn't understand and hadn't told anyone cause she thought she was going mad. I then explained what happened to me and it seemed to help her a lot. We never discussed it again after that night!

The second person is my current husband, and not so long ago at that either. I also told him how strange it was that I seem to know what is "medically" wrong, most of the time, when someone close to me is not well, and after going to the doctor and getting a diagnosis, I find that I had said that that was the problem I had come up with! I seem to instinctively "know", and in most cases, I also "know" what to do, though I always recommend the doctor!

The third person was someone at work only a few weeks ago, I don't know how it came up . . . ah yes, she was describing something "weird" as she put it that had recently happened to her. I found myself just "blurting" it all out, then I felt like a "weight" had been lifted from my shoulders. Thank goodness she received it well, we've never discussed it since.

Anyway, when my son was about 8 months old, I'd gone back to have the last of my stitches out (had quite a few), and my doctor got called out of the examination room whilst we were talking and I realized that I could read my file (that was open in front of me), and I read that I had "died" for 3 minutes whilst having my son and that the recommendation was for me not to have any more children. I haven't!

11. Another Woman in Childbirth[32]

Some of the features common to NDEs include "dark tunnel", "beautiful light", "meeting kind people", "told to return, work to do, not wanting to go back".

I was in the final stage of childbirth for my first child. I began to hear a humming sound that got louder and louder. The nurse was saying something but I couldn't hear her anymore.

The things in the room and the pain faded away, turning into a dark spinning tunnel. It seemed to be spinning. There seemed to be grooves like that of the lines on a screw nail going around the inside edges of this tunnel. It seemed like it was a large black steel cylinder. It seemed to be revolving slowly on the outside but I was spinning faster and faster as I ascended up toward the top of this cylinder. The humming sound lessened once I realized I was in this tunnel. I did not know where I was going. I remember thinking, "Where was I going?" I began to look around to see how I could get back out of it, yet at the same time don't remember looking around. I then saw a light at the opening of the top of this tunnel. This light was a small opening to begin with and then became immensely beautiful. I cannot describe this brilliant white, yellow light. It was like it was more of a feeling of peace than something to describe. I wanted to go toward it and let myself continue to travel toward it.

As I got closer to the opening the light got larger and larger like a spreading out of something spilling. There appeared the upper torsos of approximately 6 people looking into the tunnel. They reached their hands out toward me to help me get there. They were dressed in black, seemed very kindly. Just as I was almost in grasping reach of a few of their hands they pushed me back. I don't know how because they never touched me. They just kept their hands withdrawn enough so that I couldn't reach them. I remember feeling very sad because I couldn't reach them.

I seemed to be asking them to help me get to them but not with words from my mouth. They said "No you have to go back, you have something to do, you can't come right now, it's not time yet for you to come"—words something to that effect. I remember them looking at me but they had no faces. Yet I think they were old relatives and I know for sure one of them was an old uncle that died when I was a child. As they withdrew their hands back into the light, I momentarily felt bad as my hands began to drift back down the tunnel. I didn't want to go back. I remember going up toward the light but it seemed like I only remember my hands retreating backward down the tunnel.

The next thing I remember I was in the delivery room and a nurse was slapping the tops of my hands quite hard and saying "Hey wake up there, you have a beautiful baby girl." I forgot this incident for many years or rather just never talked about it. I don't know which.

12. Life Review Effects

This is the account of a man who died, went to the other side, and learned a great deal. After he returned, he began to analyse his experience and attempted to understand all that he learned. He shares many interesting insights, especially what he learned from his life review. At one point, though, he realised that living his life was what he was supposed to do, at least while his children were young. Recently he has begun again his quest to understand. Perhaps one day we will hear how he brings religion and science together.[33]

His "big event'', as he describes it, happened one night when he and his wife were visiting Oregon and stayed the night in an old motel with horrible soft mattresses. Halfway through the night he slipped off the mattress and got wedged between mattress and wall, provoking an apnoea attack which sent him into some form of cardiac failure.

What happened next, he admits, sounds reminiscent of science fiction, but he feels he cannot emphasise too strongly that his NDE, which followed, actually happened. Once again we meet an experiencer who is certain about the reality of his experience. One can ask, why would anybody go to such trouble to have their experience publicised unless they were convinced that it was "real"?

He said that he did not experience the usual components of near death experiences he had read about, such as out-of-body observation of himself. Rather he was blasted through an amazing tunnel of brightness which brought him ever closer to an unbelievably bright light, a place overwhelmingly bright and swimming with "fluid colours of the entire spectrum".

At first he didn't realise that he was without his physical body until he found he could not see his hands, and consequently was not happy about it, so much so that he started screaming in a voice which he could hear in his head but could not physically perceive. He thought: "No f***cking way, I'm not finished yet, I have young children, I have not seen my life through yet! No damn it!" He continued with the verbal abuse of any one who was listening in very profane language until he heard a voice say "OK, relax. It's not your time."

He knew at that moment, two very clear truths to be real, first that he was not going to die yet (or stay dead if he was already dead!). Secondly, there was a God and an afterlife beyond our life on earth. But unlike other near death experiencers whom he had read about he didn't see or feel the presence of Jesus, or Buddha, or Allah, nor the physical presence of relatives who had passed on before him—although he did have a strong feeling that they were with him.

What he did see was a much brighter place nearby that seemed to pull at his heart to come closer. Whenever he looked in the direction of this "portal" as he described it, he was awash with a complete feeling of peace, calm and contentment, However he realised that moving into the portal would mean that he would be unable to return to his life on earth which he so desperately wanted.

Suddenly a conversation took place that changed his life. "You are troubled", a voice said. "Your need to know the truth about your life, it is holding you back from living your life to the fullest." Without speaking, he agreed, and knew that the voice was that of Whom he understood to be God, and that the communication was coming, in his words, "from all that is, all that was, all that ever shall be."

He was told by the voice that if he wanted to be happy he must first know what he needed to change about his life on earth. In an instant he was seeing his life in review, first of all the wonderful feelings that had brought joy into his life, the incredible events when love was most present in his life, childhood memories, first real loves, the first time that he knew he loved the woman who was to be his wife, and births of his children. But then came the other side of his life, but it came as surprise that it was not the lying and deceit of his youth nor the trysts and dalliances from his college days, rather "the times that I had hurt others to such a degree as to make them doubt their self-worth, or their ability to love and be loved". Girls he had slammed and disrespected in his college days, people who had admired him only to be disrespected or even worse, ignored when they reached out a hand in friendship. People who had been harmed by his "cutting sarcasm and smart-ass wit"; callous remarks or actions that at the time seemed inconsequential, the thoughtless acts of impulse that were dismissed by his cocky self-assured attitude.

His review was one of self judgement, a commonly reported component of near death experiences.

But even with this primary evidence in front of him the only question which remained in his head was: "Why? What does it all mean?" And that was when he made a mistake which almost ruined his life—because the answer to his questions was: Must you really know these answers in order to be able to enjoy life on earth? He replied emphatically in the affirmative.

Instantly he was blasted with a force of "knowledge", powerful and overwhelming. He said he was suddenly faced with all of the answers to life, to death, to science and theology, and all of the amazing intricacies of their interaction. At this point he awoke, terrified in the darkness, by all this knowledge. His wife awoke asking him what was wrong but he was terrified to speak of what he had just experienced, that he had just died, so he decided not to tell her, it was a secret he concealed from her for months while he tried to work out what had happened. Keeping that secret, he realised later when he did tell her, was a breach of trust on his part, which she resented.

In the instant he returned from his "little trip to the other side", as he was later affectionately to call it, he knew several things to be true.

Most importantly that it was real, it did happen. There could be no other explanation for the onslaught of information that he now possessed, and now coursing through his mind; facts about things which he had never studied, nor even had the remotest interest in, such as physics, quantum mechanics, and the balance between positive and negative energy; for him it was a verification of the very existence of something beyond this life.

For almost two years he was rendered almost completely without any other purpose, by the quest to try and understand the answer to his question "Why?"—the why of that gift he had been given. On and on, he said, until he thought he would go mad grappling with that question, rendering everything he did inconsequential and meaningless.

Then, he was saved from this state of mind by his children, the eldest eleven at the time.

One bright sunny Saturday morning while he was reading a book about the correlation between time, space and religion, in his eternal quest, they asked him if he would take them to the park. He snapped at them telling them that he was busy and had things to do. Their response overwhelmed him as they replied "It's OK, we still love you—we'll wait for you!"

(I know the effect it would have had on him as I went through a similar experience with one of my children when I apologised on one occasion for losing my temper and behaving like a "mad dog". I received an almost identical response: that it was OK, "I know that you love me", prompting an immediate rethink in my attitudes.)

In that moment he was so filled with emotion and love that he finally understood the real answers to life. He realised that all the things that really mattered, truth, love, happiness, honesty were embodied in the simple phrase "with the love of a child".

Since then he found himself increasingly wanting to be involved in the sufferings of close friends and relatives many of whom had died of cancer or accidents, realising that it was his role to give comfort to the grieving, and that it was to perform that role that he had been given back his life.

13. Jamey Massengale

The case of Jamey is particularly important, for his experience occurred due to an allergic drug reaction while serving a twenty year sentence in prison. His account was submitted to P.M.H. Atwater. It is significant because not only does he recount having met Jesus but also gives a description of him which exactly matches three letters written at the time Jesus lived, i.e. red, or red-gold hair, soft, grey or blue eyes, and that he was unusually tall.[34]

His account follows:

> I was in a cell alone and I recall not breathing for a long time, and thinking that was very strange. I began to experience what others who have had NDEs call "nothingness." It made me feel powerful as though

I were God, and that space and time were at my disposal . . . and then I heard a voice that said, "What is it that you want?"

Where was this voice coming from, and what does it mean when it asks, what do I want? But then emotion began to well up inside me and I felt heartbreak like I had never felt before in my life, and the words just poured out of my mouth: "I just want to know if Jesus is real?" Then the voice said very matter-of-factly: "Yes, he is."

I was then transported up into the most beautiful open plain I had ever seen in my life, where I could see the inside of everything that grew there, and in the distance was a beautiful crystal city. I immediately began to fly toward it, but before I got to the city, I began to go up into the clouds. As I looked above me, the clouds were glowing golden. They rolled back, parting like we imagine the Red Sea parted before Moses, and there stood Jesus.

There two men, dark men, who looked like desert prophets wearing sackcloth, standing on either side of him. Jesus was wearing shining light. His skin seemed to glow with the light, and it came from his beautiful blue eyes. He had fiery red hair. He asked me; "Are you ready to come in? I said; "No, I want to stay and help others. He said with a smile: "When you are ready you can come in".

And then I was back in my body, back in the cell, back in prison, and in the beginnings of a new adventure such as I could never have imagined.

14. A Neurosurgeon

Dr Eben Alexander graduated from the University of North Carolina in 1976 with a major in chemistry and earned his MD at Duke University Medical School in 1988. During his eleven years at medical school and residency training at Duke, Massachusetts General Hospital, and Harvard, he focussed on the subject of neuroendocrinology.

After completing a fellowship in cerebrovascular neurosurgery at Newcastle-Upon-Tyne in England he spent fifteen years as an Associate Professor of Surgery at the Harvard Medical School, specialising in neurosurgery and operating on countless patients many with severe life-threatening brain conditions. Learning about the workings of the human body and brain was his life's calling, hence the importance of his near death experience in relation to the question of the reality, as challenged by many sceptics, of NDEs.

On November 10, 2008, at the age of fifty-four, Alexander was struck by a rare illness, later proved to be a near fatal form of meningitis, and thrown into a coma for seven days. He said, and wrote, of it:[35]

> During that time, my entire neocortex—the outer surface of the brain, the part that makes us human—was shut down. Inoperative. In essence, absent. When your brain is absent, you are absent, too. As a neurosurgeon, I'd heard many stories over the years of people who had strange experiences, usually after suffering cardiac arrest: stories of traveling to mysterious, wonderful landscapes; of talking to dead relatives—even of meeting God Himself. Wonderful stuff, no question. But all of it, in my opinion, pure fantasy.
>
> When the machine (i.e. brain) breaks down, consciousness stops. As vastly complicated and mysterious as the actual mechanics of brain processes are, in essence the matter is as simple as that. Pull the plug and the TV goes dead. The show is over, no matter how much you might have been enjoying it.
>
> Or so I would have told you before my own brain crashed.
>
> As a practising neurosurgeon with decades of research and hands-on work in the operating room behind me, I was in a better than average position to judge not only the reality but also the implications of what happened to me.
>
> These implications are tremendous beyond description.
> My experience showed me that the death of the body and brain are not the end of consciousness, that human experience continues beyond the grave.
>
> More important, it continues under the gaze of a God who loves and cares for each one of us.
>
> The place I went to was real.
>
> Real in a way that makes the life we are living here and now dreamlike by comparison. That doesn't mean I don't value the life I'm

> living now however. In fact I value it more than I ever did before. I do so because I see it in its true context.
>
> This life isn't meaningless. But we can't see that from here—at least most of the time. What happened to me while I was in that coma is the most important story I will ever tell. But it's a tricky story to tell because it is so foreign to ordinary understanding.
>
> At the same time my conclusions are based upon a medical analysis of my experience, and on my familiarity with most advanced concepts in brain science. Once I realised the truth behind my journey, I knew I had to tell it. Doing so properly has become the chief task of my life.
>
> That does not mean that I have abandoned my medical work and my life as neurosurgeon. But now that I have been privileged to understand that our life does not end with the death of the body or the brain, I see it as my duty, my calling, to tell people what I saw beyond the body and beyond this earth.
>
> I am especially eager to tell my story to the people who might have heard stories similar to mine before and wanted to believe them, but had not fully been able to do so.

His NDE: while in his comatose state he began by finding himself in a "creepy" place, timeless and boundaryless, but he felt he wasn't part of that subterranean world, but was trapped in it. Whatever or whoever he was he didn't belong there, and needed to get out.

As he asked that question something new emerged from the darkness above him, something that wasn't cold, or dark, or dead. Rather the exact opposite of those things.

He said that if he tried for the rest of his life he would never be able to do justice to the entity which now approached him—to come anywhere close to describing how beautiful it was—but he had to try.

In a flash Alexander found himself in a completely new world, the most beautiful he had ever seen—brilliant, vibrant, ecstatic, stunning. He said he was flying, passing over trees and fields, streams and waterfalls, and here and there, people, children too, laughing and playing. The people sang and danced around in circles, and sometimes he saw a dog running and jumping among them.

A beautiful, incredible dream world, he said—except it wasn't a dream. Though he didn't know where he was he was absolutely sure that this place in which he found himself was completely real.

He asked readers and listeners to remember who was talking to them now. He wasn't a soft-hearted sentimentalist, he knew what death looked like; he knew what it was like to have a living person become a lifeless object on an operating table after one has struggled for hours to keep the machine of the body working. He knew what suffering looked like, and the answerless grief on the faces of loved ones who have lost someone they had never dreamed they could lose.

Most importantly, he knew his biology, he knew the difference between fantasy and reality, and he knew that his experience was the single most important of his life.

Dr Alexander's account continues along these lines: At some point he realised that he wasn't alone up there; a beautiful girl with high cheek bones and deep blue eyes was next to him who "spoke" to him without using any words.

He instantly however understood her message which he said if he had to translate into earthly language would run something like this:

"You are loved and cherished, dearly, forever"

"You have nothing to fear"

"There is nothing you can do wrong"

In his one word—love. Which was what he learned, and which was the basis of everything, in its purest form—unconditional, the reality of realities, the core of everything that exists or will exist

The girl said that he would be shown many things while in that place, but eventually he would have to go back. But back where, he asked himself?

And return to this life he eventually did via the first "hellish" place he had visited in his NDE, but which he now understood the importance of, in that our lives must be ruled by love, otherwise that place will be the starting point for upward spiritual growth.

After his return to this life, Alexander took an interest in Raymond Moody's book which had led to the formation of IANDS. Whereas previously he had discounted his stories and had never opened it, as he knew that they were fantasy, he now read them with reference of what he had gone through, and found the similarities with what he himself had experienced quite overwhelming.

15. Father Richard Neuhaus

Just as I have chosen case studies from several medical people because of widespread scepticism among that profession as to the reality of NDEs, so too I have I chosen the following case study because of similar attitudes amongst many clergy, who are well known for using the argument of "nothing about that in the Bible"—when of course there certainly is something in the Bible. Most telling is that story Jesus tells of Dives and Lazarus, and the different states they find themselves in after death. But I have also chosen him because he was one of the most prominent and respected intellectuals in America, and the author of several acclaimed books.

Richard Neuhaus was originally a Lutheran Pastor but was received into the Roman Catholic Church in 1990 and a year later ordained a priest in the Archdiocese of New York. He served as a commentator for the Catholic television network Eternal World Television during the funeral of Pope John Paul II and the election of Pope Benedict XVI, and he was an unofficial adviser on ethical and religious matters to President George W. Bush. He was president of the "Institute on Religion and Public Life", and the author of several acclaimed books. "U.S. News and World Report" considered him: "one of the most influential intellectuals in America".

Further Neuhaus admits he was one of those clergy who were

sceptical about near death experiences; however he felt very differently about them following his own.

He was in hospital following three operations. Two days after leaving the intensive care unit he could hear patients in adjoining rooms moaning and mumbling and occasionally calling out when all of a sudden he was jerked into an utterly lucid state of awareness when he realised staring into the darkness at some hanging drapery he saw beside it two "presences". He said of them:[36]

> And then the presences—one or both of them, I do not know—spoke. Then I heard clearly, not in an ordinary way, but the message was beyond mistaking: "Everything is ready now"—it was not in the form of a command , nor was it an invitation to do anything—they were just letting me know. That was it. They waited for a while, maybe a minute, maybe for longer, then they were gone.

This led to his most important comment:

> Had I been dreaming? No way. I was then and am now as lucid and wide awake as I had ever been in my life. Tell me that I was dreaming and you might as well tell me that I was dreaming that I wrote the sentence before this one. I resolved at that moment I would never, never, let anything dissuade me from the reality of what I had experienced. It was any experience as real, as powerful, as anything I have ever known.

Neuhaus would be thinking about "everything is ready now" incessantly during the months of his convalescence; his theological mind would go to work on it and he realised that his messengers were angels, which is what the word angel means. There were no white robes or wings or anything of that sort, merely a message—a message that he could go somewhere with them.

> Go where? To God or so it seemed. I understood that they were ready to get me ready to see God. But it was obvious that I was not prepared in my present physical and spiritual condition for the beatific vision of seeing God face to face. They were ready to get me ready. This is consistent with the Roman Catholic doctrine of purgatory[37] that there

is a process of purging and preparation to get us ready to meet God. The decision was mine as to when or whether I would take them up on the offer.

What happened to me on that hospital bed was, of course, no world class apparition . . . it was a word very personally addressed to me. To judge what many others say, it was not even so extraordinary, at least not in terms of the frequency of such things happening. More than a third of adult Americans say that they have at some point in their lives received communications from angels, saints, or even God himself, and at least on the surface many reports bear similarities to mine.

(I found this to be so in Australia, too, following an address I gave on NDEs at Bowral, NSW, to an audience of approximately 200 people. I was quite amazed at the number of them who came up to me afterwards to tell me of similar experiences.)

Neuhaus continued:

> Presumably I had not yet died; the experience was on the near side of death, but there has always been a Christian tradition along with Plato and the best of the ancients, that death when it occurs is followed by judgment, a prospect that is not unattended by fear, even terror, yet the message I received was so very friendly and consoling, as though a positive outcome of the judgment was confidently expected.
>
> Is it possible that death is part of life, or even that death is not death at all? Is it possible that, between this world and the next, we simply move from life to life? I know what I understood by the announcement to me that night. If I chose to go with them something would happen between here and where we were going, and that something is called death. I did not take that next step but it was my choice.

16. A Carpenter's NDE

Just as I started these case studies with a "classic" NDE, so do I finish them with another one of somebody returning to life after having been declared clinically dead. One which can fairly claim to be the truly "classic" NDE—that of a humble, thirty three year old carpenter's son, Jesus of Nazareth. That he was clinically dead is confirmed by the fact that the Roman soldiers did not break his legs on the cross. It was their custom to remove dead

John Bowers, who became head of the United Nations Literacy Programme, served as an officer in the Sudan during World War II. The near death experience which followed an attack by German bombers had a significance that led him to see it as part of his 'training course for life'. Along with Nita McCallum's, his experience is related by Peter and Elizabeth Fenwick in their book, *The Truth in the Light: An Investigation of Over 300 Near Death Experiences.*

Nita McCallum was devoutly Roman Catholic at the time of her NDE in 1972. The experience seemed unrelated to her Catholicism, and rather than reinforcing specific articles of faith it widened horizons for her.

bodies from a cross at sunset, but if any were found still alive the legs would be broken, an action which would almost immediately kill the victim.

Jesus's death is referred to daily in the definitive creeds of the Christian Church, in particular the Nicene Creed of AD 381 and the following is the relevant section of that creedal statement:

> And was made man, and was crucified for us under Pontius Pilate.
> He suffered and was buried.
> And the third day he rose again according to the Scriptures.[38]

What are the facts about the life of Jesus? That he lived and was sentenced to death for what was deemed blasphemy by the Jews, i.e. equating himself as one with God. And there is overwhelming evidence for the objective observer that he did die following his crucifixion and that he did return to life after three days (which I will endeavour to substantiate in a later chapter).

Further, not only did he return from death but there were about 500 people, according to St. Paul, (the same St. Paul who had previously been one of Jesus's persecutors prior to his mystical "Road to Damascus" experience), as well as the disciples, who had seen him and could verify his bodily return as truth.

Accepting this, as the Christian does, makes anything Jesus said about the reality of an afterlife critical.

CHAPTER 6

Deathbed Visions: Another Form of Near Death Experience

A deathbed vision is a frequently reported or observed phenomenon when someone close to death sees a vision of a deceased loved one, or loved ones, who greet them to help the dying make the transition through death. These often occur even days before that transition.

An example in my own experience came from a parishioner, who knowing of my interest in the subject of NDEs, and whose husband was a fellow priest, wrote to me and told me of his transition.

She said he had been terminally ill, had had constant palliative care in the few weeks leading up to his departure, and had been in a coma for several days prior to it.

On what was to prove his final day she had got into bed with him to embrace him and lay with him for several hours, until suddenly, without warning, he had sat bolt upright in bed and called out in a loud voice "O Mother!" then lay back and died.

Woman Dying in Childbirth

Dr Carla Wills-Brandon has written an excellent book *One Last Hug Before I Go* in which she identifies Sir William Barrett, a physics professor at the Royal College of Science in Dublin, as the first to study deathbed visions in scientific literature, even though they had been commonly reported, as the author claims, in general "literature and lore of all ages." He would never have considered examining such a topic except for an experience told to him by his wife, an obstetric surgeon, who had been called into the operating room to deliver the child of a woman, who, in spite of her child being delivered healthy, was dying from haemorrhage. As Lady Barrett told her husband:

> Suddenly she looked eagerly towards part of the room, a radiant smile illuminating her whole countenance.
>
> "Oh, lovely, lovely," she said.
>
> I asked, "What is lovely"
>
> "What I see," she replied in low, intense tones.
>
> "What do you see?"
>
> "Lovely brightness—wonderful beings."
>
> Then, seeming to focus her attention more intently on one place, she exclaimed almost with a kind of joyous cry:
>
> "Why, it's Father! Oh, he's so glad I am coming; he is so glad."

Although the story was compelling, sceptics could argue that it was nothing more than a hallucination due to lack of blood or fear of death, a point which Sir William possibly made to his wife, until he heard the rest of the story. The patient, Doris, had a sister Vida, who had died only three weeks earlier. Vida's death had been kept secret from Doris because of her delicate condition which is why her deathbed vision was so amazing to Barrett.

After recognising her father, Doris spoke to him saying that she was coming and that he was so near, but then with a rather puzzled expression said: "He has Vida with him."

Could all this merely have been wish fulfilment expressed in the form of a hallucination? Barrett considered such an explanation, but he rejected it because among the apparitions of the dead was someone whom Doris had not expected to see—Vida, whose appearance was a surprise to Doris who was unaware of her death. This story was so inspirational to Barrett that he undertook a systematic study of deathbed visions. His was the first scientific study to conclude that the mind of the dying patient is often clear and rational.

A Young Boy's Deathbed Vision

Carla Wills-Brandon's research also reveals the story of a young boy, related by his mother, of her child's deathbed visions:

> Our son passed over on August 4, 1997. I believe he did have deathbed visions. The first one happened after he had a seizure. His heart stopped, and after he came back to life, he seemed all right. But then he looked at me and said:
>
> "Mum, what happened to me?"
>
> I didn't want to scare him, so I told him he had fainted. He replied:
>
> "Whatever happened to me was wonderful, it felt so good. I liked that."
>
> When my husband visited with the doctor he told him what our son had said and the doctor said to him: "You do know that what your son experienced was a near death experience?"
>
> When the second vision took place, my son had been unconscious for over an hour. Suddenly, he sat up in an upright position! This happened very quickly. We were so shocked, we didn't say a word to him. We thought, "My God, he came out of it!" so we just sat and stared.
>
> He looked toward the foot of his bed and then up. He was looking as though he were seeing more than one person. He turned his head slightly from side to side. The look on his face was like he was confused with what he was staring at. Then, after a few minutes, he laid back down and looked very peaceful. He returned to his unconscious state and at this point all we could do was hold him. Not long after that, our son went into cardiac arrest and passed on.

Another Young Boy

The following deathbed account was told to Professor Melvin Morse by a physician in Utah.

> A five-year-old boy, dying from a malignant brain tumor, had been in the coma for three weeks and was surrounded almost the entire time by his family. They encircled his bed and prayed constantly for his recovery, taking only brief breaks to eat and rest. At the end of the third week, the pastor of the family's church came into the hospital room and told them a remarkable story. He'd had a dream, he said, in which

> the boy told him: "It's my time to die. You must tell my parents to quit praying. I am supposed to go now." The pastor was nervous about delivering this message to the family. Still, he said, it was a message too vivid to ignore.

The family members accepted the minister's dream as a message from their son. They prayed, they touched his comatose body, and they told him that he would be missed, but he had permission to die.

Suddenly, the boy regained consciousness. He thanked his family for letting him go and told them he would be dying soon. He died the next day.

Perhaps the most important aspect of this story is its cathartic nature. This family was allowed to assuage its grief because they knew that their son was ready to die. Their resentment of life's process and of God's will was replaced by the assurance that something mystical had taken place.

A Deathbed Vision in Sydney: Nelly Stephen

Sir Alfred Stephen in the mid-19th century was Chief Justice of New South Wales; also, what is known today as Rector's Warden, at Christ Church, St. Laurence, Sydney.

In the south wall of the sanctuary of Christ Church are two memorial windows erected by Sir Alfred: one to Lady Stephen's mother, Eleanor Bedford, the other to one of the Stephens' daughters, also Eleanor but known as Nelly.

Nelly died in 1861, a young woman. The family diary records that one of the family went off to tell the grandmother that her granddaughter had just died, but the grandmother sat up in bed and said firmly: "She shall not go alone," feeling no doubt that Nelly was too young to take such a long journey unattended. "I see her walking in the golden street," said Grandmama in her dying trance, and so set out on the same far journey![39]

Here we have, probably, the first record in Sydney of a near death experience in the form of a deathbed vision, a phenomenon which attracts considerable attention today.

Saul of Tarsus

I suggest that probably the most famous vision occurred to St. Paul, as he became known, not on his deathbed, but on the road to Damascus. Luke, who accompanied Paul on many missionary voyages, in the Acts of the Apostles—the sequel to his Gospel—refers to his vision in detail in Acts on two occasions.[40]

First, he sets the scene prior to his vision at the time of the stoning to death of the first Christian martyr, Stephen (Acts 8:1–3).

> And Saul approved of their killing him. That day a severe persecution began against the church in Jerusalem, and all except the apostles were scattered throughout the countryside of Judea and Samaria. Devout men buried Stephen and made loud lamentation over him, but Saul was ravaging the church by entering house after house, dragging off both men and women, and committing them to prison.

Then his vision:

> Meanwhile Saul, still breathing threats and murder against the disciples of the Lord went to the high priest and asked him for letters to the synagogues at Damascus so that if he found any who belonged to the Way, he might bring them bound to Jerusalem.
>
> Now as he was going along and approaching Damascus suddenly a light from heaven flashed around him. He fell to the ground and heard a voice saying "Saul, Saul, why do you persecute me?" He asked: "Who are you Lord?" The reply came "I am Jesus whom you are persecuting. But get up and enter the city and you will be told what to do."
>
> The men who were travelling with him were speechless because they heard the voice but saw no one. Saul got up from the ground and though his eyes were open he could see nothing, so they led him by hand and took him to Damascus.
>
> For three days he was without sight and neither ate nor drank.

The outcome of this experience for Saul, as described in Acts 9:19–22, was:

> For several days he was with the disciples in Damascus and immediately began to proclaim Jesus in the synagogues, saying: "He is the Son

of God." All who heard him were amazed and said: "Is not this the man who made havoc in Jerusalem and has he not come here for the purpose of bringing them bound before the chief priests?"

Saul became increasingly more powerful and confounded the Jews who lived in Damascus by proving that Jesus was the Messiah.

Several points should be noted about Paul's vision. First, that his companions saw nothing as with other visions referred to previously. Second, the power of that vision—which changed his life and proved the reality, I suggest, of his NDE. Third, the nature of the vision, i.e. surrounded by light, which will lead us into the next level of enquiry—the role of "the Light".

CHAPTER 7

The Light

> Rank on rank the host of heaven spreads its vanguard on the way.
> As the light of light descendeth from the realms of endless day.
> That the powers of hell may vanish as the darkness clears away.
>
> —"Let all Mortal Flesh Keep Silence" (hymn)

"Have you been to the Light?" That was the question asked of me by the man who was my first face to face encounter with somebody who had had a profound near death experience. The man showed traces of a fearful wound in his head (healed), presumably the cause of his NDE, and was one of many to whom I have referred, those who had come a long way at considerable personal expense to attend the annual IANDS conference held that year in Vancouver, Canada. His tone was so reverential.

THE LIGHT OF THE WORLD

If one particular theme stands out, above all others, as revealed in studies of NDEs, it is that of "light" or "being of light"; it is the most profound because of its effect upon the experiencer. Sometimes it is referred to only as a presence, by others it is identified as a particular being, but always in the context of intense peace and love.

The following extracts are from Chapter 5.

Ian Cochrane described it thus:

"I knew I was going 'there' walking towards the 'sun', which drew me towards it with its inviting glow and warmth, the most delightful yellowish colour imaginable." He ended his account with an exhortation suitable for the others which follow: "I am able to tell people close to death 'welcome it', it's going to be the best experience ever . . . Rejoice."

Howard Storm

When Howard Storm screamed into the darkness "Jesus save me": "a faint star appeared in the darkness, growing rapidly until soon it was an indescribably brilliant light becoming brighter and brighter." Which light Storm called the "Angel of Light".

Patient of Dr Moody

Who said she came out of the dark tunnel "into a realm of soft brilliant light. The love was everywhere, it surrounded me and seemed to soak into my very being and people I knew who had died were there with me in the light."

The medical doctor:

"who took my hand and guided me toward a tunnel at the end of the tunnel was glowing white light . . . where I experienced complete and cosmic peace. I was in the presence of a very calming loving formless bluish light, an entity, which I somehow knew or felt was supreme love, knowledge and intelligence personified." Later as he was returning to this life directed by his father, "I came out into a place of profound calmness, light and joy. I was greeted by two beings who were like young men, radiating energy and light, full of vigour, enthusiasm and love who told me they were angels . . . they told me that they were my guardian angels."

He then found himself "immersed in a formless, shapeless Blue Light. The Light Being began 'speaking' to me but I heard the words as if through a gentle wind that was whispering to me in my ear. The Light Being seemed to be diffused throughout this entire dimension. It is hard to describe in words how it felt to be in the presence of the Light Being: PURE LOVE pervaded everything, as if all the five earthly senses were soaked in love. It was present everywhere, all powerful.

My consciousness felt merged with the supreme primordial consciousness. I was at once communicating with It and in It. The closer, or more connected I had become to the Light Being, the clearer and more intensified the chant in the distance had become."

Helen during her attempted suicide:

"Then I remember a very powerful force pulling me towards a serene, very beautiful realm, a higher realm. I traveled very slowly along a tunnel toward a bright light, and I could feel an overwhelming sense of warmth and peace and whiteness. I wanted to walk into the whiteness, which was so tranquil and happy."

The NDE of a child

The case of Robin Michelle Halberdier of Texas City, Texas, illustrates the overwhelming sense of love experiencers often encounter in the light. She remembers the near death episode that took place in a hospital when she was between one and two months of age. Born prematurely, and with hyaline membrane disease, she was not expected to live.[41]

> My first visual memory was looking forward and seeing a brilliant bright light, almost like looking directly at the sun. The strange thing was that I could see my feet in front of me, as if I were floating upward in a vertical position. I do not remember passing through a tunnel or anything like that, just floating in the beautiful light. A tremendous amount of warmth and love came from the light.
>
> There was a figure standing in the light, shaped like a normal human being, but with no distinct facial features. It had a masculine presence. The light I have described seemed like it emanated from that figure. Light rays shone all around him. I felt very protected and safe and loved.
>
> The figure in the light told me through what I now know to be mental telepathy that I must go back, that it was not time for me to come here. I wanted to stay because I felt so full of joy and so peaceful. The voice repeated that it wasn't my time; I had a purpose to fulfill and I could come back after I completed it.
>
> "The first time I told my parents about my experience was right after I began to talk. At the time, I believed that what happened to me was something everyone experienced. I told my mom and dad about the big glass case I was in after I was born, and the figure in the light and what he said to me. They took my reference to the glass case to mean

the incubator. My father was a medical student at the time, and he had read a book about near death experiences. From comparing the information in the book with what I told them, they decided that's what I was describing. My mom told me all of this years later when I brought the subject up again.

I began attending church at the age of five, and I would look at the picture of Jesus in the Bible and tell my mom that's who it was in the light. I still have many physical difficulties with my health because of being premature. But there is a strong need inside me that I should help others with what death is, and talk to terminally ill patients. I was in the other world and I know there is nothing to be afraid of after death.

Tibetan Buddhist: Lingza Chokyi's Near Death Experience

Here we find the same theme of light as with other NDEs, differing only in its identification.

In the bardo of becoming, as well as many other kinds of visions, the mental body will see visions and signs of different realms. A small percentage of those who have survived a NDE describe visions of inner worlds, paradises, and cities of light with transcendental music. The teaching is: "O son/daughter of an enlightened family . . . your Rigpa is inseparable luminosity and emptiness and dwells as a great expanse of light; beyond birth or death, it is, in fact, the Buddha of Unchanging Light.

THE CHRISTIAN PERSPECTIVE

That different interpretation of the identity of the Light in many NDEs, e.g. Buddha as above, and Jesus by many Christians, or no identification at all, invites serious investigation.

From a Christian perspective the prologue to John's Gospel makes an important statement by John the Baptist about John's role as a witness to the Light without giving Him any identity other than "The Word".

This is the *New Revised Standard Version* translation of the Prologue:

In the beginning was the Word, and the Word was with God, and the Word was God.

> All things came into being through Him, and without Him not one thing came into being.
>
> What has come into being in him was life, and the life was the light of all people.
>
> The light shines in the darkness, and the darkness did not overcome it.
>
> There was a man sent from God, whose name was John.
>
> He came as a witness to testify to the light, so that all might believe through him.
>
> He himself was not the light, but he came to testify to the light.
>
> The true light, which enlightens every one was coming into the world.
>
> He was in the world, and the world came into being through Him; yet the world did not know Him.
>
> He came to his own people, but his own people did not accept him.

This insistence upon the light as a mission to all people (not just the Jewish race) and that the world came into being through Him is redolent of the wise saying: "There is only one God, but He has many different names."

Allah? God? Jehovah? Yahweh? Buddha?

Either God is, or God isn't, but it is fanciful to suggest there can be more than one God, perfectly reasonable however to say that different religious faiths have different interpretations of the nature of Him Whom the Christian knows as "God".

From the Christian perspective, John's Gospel is most informative because of the things Jesus claims for Himself.[42] So much so that it is often referred to as the "I Am" Gospel, in particular that He was the Light of the World (John 8:12), reminding one of C.S. Lewis's statement about he, Lewis, being able to see only three alternatives about Jesus: mad, a liar, or Who He said He was.

When one considers Jesus's claims as recorded in John's "I am" gospel, and the evidence of His miraculous deeds which generated vast crowds following Him everywhere for three years, hearing His teachings, and witnessing those healing miracles, I know which one of C.S. Lewis's alternatives breathes truth for me.

And it was neither a madman, nor a liar.

CHAPTER 8

Spirits in Divine Service

Further evidence, I suggest, for belief in an afterlife may be found from research into the existence and life of angels.

The Bible, for example, is full of encounters with angels. Celestial beings are referred to 196 times, 103 times in the Old Testament and 93 times in the New Testament, important as it shows belief in a higher mode of existence, by both Judaism and Christianity, which humankind may eventually inherit, the life of the world to come.

There are references right from the beginning of creation with the Fall of Adam and Eve. In Genesis 3:23–24 we read:

> The Lord God therefore banished him from the garden of Eden, to till the ground from which he had been taken. When he expelled the man, he settled him east of the garden of Eden; and he stationed the cherubim and the fiery revolving sword, to guard the way to the tree of life.

Also in Genesis, Jacob's dream of the ladder to heaven and the angels of God ascending and descending on it. Then in Exodus 23:20–22 God sends an angel to lead Moses out of the wilderness to the promised land. And in Daniel, when the lions refused to eat Daniel, he cries:

> My God sent his angel and shut the lions' mouths, and they have not hurt me because I was found blameless before him. (6:19–22)

ANGELS IN THE CHRISTIAN TRADITION

We find angels present at Jesus' birth, and two angels outside the tomb in the garden at his resurrection, and by the time we arrive at the last page of scripture we have had so many encounters with angels they have become like old friends.

We read in the Gospels how after Jesus' temptation by the devil in the wilderness the angels came and ministered to Him, and how when Jesus sent his disciples out to preach and heal He told them that the angels would protect them. And, in Hebrews, we learn that angels not only serve Jesus, but also us, for the passage declares: "Are not angels spirits in the divine service, sent to serve those who are to inherit salvation?"

THE BOOK OF REVELATION

In Revelation, John and his angel guide saunter together by the river of life and take in the grandeur of the Holy City, but the angel is quite alarmed when John falls down to worship him, insisting that he is nothing more than a fellow servant of God along with John and all the prophets. And then there's John's description in Revelation of the angels worshipping God.

Also in Revelation we are told of war in heaven as the great archangels gather their forces against one of their own, Lucifer, or Satan, the rebel archangel. Michael and Satan ride to battle and Michael triumphs, banishing Satan and hurling him from heaven into the depths of hell.

Nevertheless, Satan still possesses grandeur and power because he is still an archangel, albeit a fallen one, and he continues to exercise his power among human beings because they are naive enough to believe he has been defeated. Indeed his most potent weapon is convincing us that he doesn't exist. But we know that he does. We know how he seduces us, as Paul so well expresses it, "I do the things that I would not, and do not do the things that I would." And who of us cannot say Amen to that?

So we may see angels as spiritual beings created by God to serve Him, though created higher than mankind. Some, the good angels, have remained obedient to Him and carry out His will, while others, the fallen angels, disobeyed, fell from their holy position, and now stand in active opposition to the work and plan of God.

JESUS VIS-A-VIS ANGELS

But most importantly for Christians—and Judaists, for after all Jesus was a Jew—is what He had to say about angels. When explaining the parable of the separation of the wheat and weeds, or tares, He says: "The Son of Man will send his angels and they will collect all evildoers out of his kingdom."

And in the same passage: "The angels will come and separate the evil from the righteous." Then speaking of the last days he says: "The Son of Man will return with his angels." Then in reference to little children: "Do not despise them, for I tell you in heaven their angels continually see the face of my Father in heaven."

He even refers in Matthew 25:41 to the devil and his angels, with the clear implication that there are bad angels as well as good angels—presumably the angels who supported Satan in his rebellion and were thrown out of heaven with him.

And recall what Jesus said at the time of His arrest: "Do you not think I cannot appeal to my Father, and he will at once send me more than twelve legions of angels?": And His story of the death of the rich man Dives and Lazarus: "The poor man died and he was carried away by the angels to be with Abraham."

And, finally, when he speaks to Nathaniel, he "who had no guile", Jesus says: "Truly I tell you, you will see heaven opened and the angels of God ascending and descending upon the Son of Man."

THE NATURE AND PURPOSE OF ANGELS

We know therefore that angels exist on a higher spiritual plane than ourselves. In Hebrews we read: "What are human beings that you are mindful of them, you have made them for a little while lower than the angels"—a most interesting statement, which implies that we have been created with the potential to be, one day, equal with the angels; that is to dwell with them in that life of the world to come.

Best of all I like that quote from Hebrews of angels, as "spirits in divine service".

J. Hampton Keathley in his book *Angelology: The Doctrine of Angels* had this to say about the creation of angels:

> Though the doctrine of angels holds an important place in the Word of God, it is often viewed as a difficult subject because, while there is abundant mention of angels in the Bible, the nature of this revelation is without the same kind of explicit description we often find with other subjects developed in the Bible.
>
> Every reference to angels is incidental to some other topic. They are not treated in themselves. God's revelation never aims at informing us regarding the nature of angels. When they are mentioned, it is always in order to inform us further about God, what he does, and how he does it. Since details about angels are not significant for that purpose, they tend to be omitted. While many details about angels are omitted, it is important to remind ourselves that celestial beings are referred to—those statistics again—196 times, in the Bible, 103 times in the Old Testament and 93 times in the New Testament.

Of course, scepticism about angels is largely a product of popular imagery of them; harps, halos, celestial choirs. And we've never seen one, yet we picture them as fiery figures with flaming swords, or fat little cherubs, depending on what time of the liturgical year we're at, and our assumption is that one day we too will be angels, claiming our halo, grabbing our harp, flapping our brilliant white wings, settling ourselves on a nice fluffy cloud, and winning a place in the heavenly choir. We have romanticised the subject through the centuries, perhaps saying too much about something we know too little.

What is the relevance of angels to us? We may assume from the biblical references that angels are messengers of God in His service, and that they are a link between heaven and earth, as exemplified by what Jesus told us in the Lazarus story: that when Lazarus died the angels came and carried him into the next life. And what a comforting thought it is that when our time comes to cross over one of these messengers of God might be waiting just as they were for Lazarus to receive us into our true home, the realm of the spirit.

And angels also come to guide, to warn, to protect us, in this life. Just think about those times in your life when you have been mysteriously guided or protected. And this principle of the mysterious, unseen angels as protectors, messengers, and guides sent by God is summed up well in Hebrews where we are advised to be on watch for their presence among us: "Do not neglect to show hospitality to strangers, for by doing that some have entertained angels without knowing it."

But there have been those times when we were aware; who, indeed, amongst us has not sensed the unseen presence of a guardian angel? Who amongst has not at some time referred, lightheartedly, perhaps, but nevertheless with some strange inner conviction, to "my guardian angel"?

Indeed, the Bible mentions guardian angels in Psalms 91:11; and Matthew 18:10: "Take heed that ye despise not one of those little ones, for I say unto you, that in heaven their angels do always behold the face of my Father which is in heaven." And Acts 12:15: "And they said unto the damsel Rhoda who was declaring Peter was at the door of Mary's house that she was mad, that it must be his angel." These give biblical authority that humans have guardian angels.

If we but keep our hearts and mind open, we will see that the angels are part of that integral connection between God and humankind, between the mysteries of heaven, and the realities of earth, his messengers and his guides, his protectors and our inner voice, and we will discern blessings ascending and descending between the human and the divine.

Angels have something important to teach us about ourselves and God. Angels remind us that our material world is influenced by the world of the spirit, and that we are intrinsically capable of inhabiting both worlds with equal ease. Humankind may rank a little lower than the angels because we are flesh as well as spirit, yet through Jesus, God's word made flesh, we can rise with the angels to share in the very life of God. Look closely and you will see that angels reveal God's secrets, guard and protect the vulnerable, are witness to miracles, and are called to unending praise.

AN ACTUAL ENCOUNTER WITH AN ANGEL

Georgina Teyrovsky wrote her story in 1989 of her near death experience involving meeting with her guardian angel, but it had taken her twenty years to find the courage and words to tell of it. She said that while in hospital with a typhus type infection in 1969, and while comatose in a critical condition, that she had had her NDE, in which she had met with, and been accompanied on, a lengthy journey by her guardian angel, from whom she learned many things:

> My guardian angel asked me what I wanted to know. I desired to see how hell and purgatory and perhaps the heavens looked. Is it something like our Catholic description indicates, fires burning, charred souls or bodies, little devils milling around?
>
> My guide (angel) smiled. I felt him smiling over my naivety. I knew he would take me there. There was no fear on my side, not even excitement. I had a feeling of detachment over my existence, my personal feelings, over the future or the past, and over my body that was left so very sick in the hospital bed. There was this sense of peace, timelessness, and trust in my guide and me.
>
> I didn't feel that my guide was illuminated or lit, but towards me a loving, caring being. I soon realised that he had been with me all of my life. Whenever I was in a difficult situation, always came this spark of thought, saving me, giving me courage, inspiring me with words and ideas which guided me out of danger and difficulty. I always thought it was because of me, my smartness, and my courage! I knew I had always had help and guidance, and I called it "good luck"![43]

Her story of her travels with her angel and what she saw and experienced is a lengthy one, but in the context of angels, suffice for the present for her to say, the most important thing she learned from her guide was:

> To learn love is the goal and purpose of existence on earth, it's about the love we feel for others, and that others feel for us. That is why it is important to pray for others, and for others to pray for us, along with our good deeds. They are the only things we take with us into the other world, into the other dimensions.

Therefore we celebrate with Georgina, not only the achievements of angels, but also the God-given potential to be one with them in the life of that "world to come".

CHAPTER 9

The Sceptics

Before proceeding it is important to explore the views of sceptics, those who advance different explanations for the near death experiences, other than "reality".

Not surprisingly near death research has faced derision, even from some religious believers who, it might have been thought, would welcome support for a principal tenet of their faith, particularly as the overwhelming majority of NDEs seem to be about love, forgiveness, and bliss.

Nevertheless, if they are real experiences as the eminent scientist and theologian Professor Father Neuhaus, among others, claim, they provide interesting information about the nature of the afterlife.

But first, the views of the sceptics.

ENDORPHIN RUSH

Chris Carter, author of *Science and The Near Death Experience,* delves at length into alternative sceptical views. One explanation involves morphine, which was first synthesised from opium in 1806 and was well received in medical circles as a great advance in pain relief. But in the 1970s it was discovered that the human body produces natural painkillers which have become known as "endorphins"—similar to morphine but produced by the body. Release of endorphins in the body has been termed an "endorphin rush" and some have suggested that this is what gives the feeling of peace and bliss during an NDE. However, this theory cannot then account for the abrupt return of pain when the NDE experience ends.

LACK OF OXYGEN

Dr Atwater, the most extensive researcher of NDEs, comments that lack of oxygen in the brain is widely offered as an explanation for causing an NDE.

Total cessation of the blood flow to the brain (anoxia), as in cardiac arrest, causes unconsciousness in seconds followed by progressive brain damage in the following three to five minutes. However, if the blood supply is not completely cut off, but merely reduced (hypoxia), then a series of "subjective" phenomena can be encountered.[44]

Studies have shown that as the brain becomes anoxic it ceases to function, and the patient becomes increasingly disorientated and confused. But this is in complete contrast to the clarity of thought and perception described over and over again in the reports of near death experiencers.

CARBON DIOXIDE

Excessive carbon dioxide in the brain is another explanation that has been proposed. This can occur through cessation of blood supply to the brain as in cardiac arrest, resulting in a rapid build-up there of carbon dioxide in the brain. However, a "failing brain, by definition, produces experiences," according to Peter Fenwick in his studies, "which are limited, confused, and disorganised." The very opposite of this is true during an NDE.[45]

REALLY DEAD?

D'Souza sees those who discount NDEs as mostly "atheists who recognise the potency and persuasive power of NDE research."[46] Their foremost argument is that the experiencers are not really dead. But many people who report NDEs—such as my first example, Ian Cochrane, in Chapter 5—are considered by the medical experts at the time to be clinically dead, showing no heart function or respiration. Today death is understood more in terms of cessation of brain, rather than heart, function, but even so van Lommel reported several NDEs that took place even after the patient's brain activity had completely ceased.[47]

CULTURAL CONDITIONING

Another refutation is that NDEs are unreliable because they are culturally conditioned. Christians tend to see Jesus, Hindus the head of an elephant, and Jews an angel or a bright light. D'Souza points out however that we would naturally interpret our experiences through a cultural lens. That a Christian might interpret a radiant being as Jesus, while a Muslim might say it's Muhammad is not surprising. No one knows what either Jesus or Muhammad looked like and as the radiant being is not "wearing a name tag" clearly the identification shows an element of cultural projection, but one cannot conclude from this that there was no radiant being or that it was simply a metaphor.

DANTE ALIGHIERI

As mentioned earlier, not every person who has been deemed clinically dead and has returned reports an NDE after resuscitation.

Kerry Packer, who famously said, after being clinically dead, that there was "nothing there" is, perhaps, an excellent example, best explained all those centuries ago by Dante when he wrote:

> I have been to that heaven where his light beams brightest and seen things that none returning has the knowledge or the power to repeat.

None has the knowledge or power to repeat.

FINAL WORD VIS-A-VIS SCEPTICS

I offer reactions of various people Dr Fenwick spoke with on a program he ran on BBC television. He said he was overwhelmed by the response he got from viewers who previously did not want to talk about their experiences, because when they tried they were often ridiculed or at best patronised, and so they gave up and kept it to themselves.

These are some of their comments about the afterlife, the reality of their experiences, and their gratitude for at last being able to discuss them.[48] You will find no sceptics among them:[49]

"You can imagine my delight when I saw your program and realised that I was not the only person who was out of step with what is termed normal."

"How thankful I am that I am not on my own with this experience."

"It's something I haven't wanted to discuss with anyone other than a few that I am very close to, but it's something I desperately want to clarify."

"Ten years ago I could not tell anyone about my experience, even my husband, because I thought people would think I was crazy."

"It comes as some relief to me to be able to actually share my experience after all these years."

"At that time, 1948, I did not mention it to anyone, in those days they would have thought that the worst had happened."

"I guess we all think others are inclined to laugh, so we keep silent."

It is also worth noting that part of the reason these people were reticent about their experiences was because they were themselves very sane ordinary people. This is what some of them said:

"I am a quite normal, level-headed human being in my forties, and yet this certainly happened to me."

"Before I tell you what happened I must tell you that my husband was a tool and die maker and tool designer. He was not a man given to fantasy, very down to earth, very honest and straightforward, an extremely hard worker, well read and intelligent."

"My friends are mostly shipyard workers or local miners, so you will understand why I have not attempted to tell anyone of my experiences; one does not discuss the idea of afterlife and reincarnation with coalminers and shipyard workers, not if one wants to keep one's friends and sanity; football, women, and greyhounds perhaps, but not the afterlife!"

Chapter 10

Beyond Blind Faith

I believe that the Christian view of Jesus as the son of God is true as proved by his resurrection. But more is needed from Christians than faith. Faith is vital for that is what makes one a Christian, but one must also be able to defend the resurrection intellectually.

Without the resurrection there is no Christian religion, it is the linchpin, it is pivotal—in Paul's words, without it "our faith is in vain." If Jesus' resurrection were not fact, nothing he had to say about eternal life could be seriously considered—nor would there be any point in studying the revelations of NDEs as to what light they might shed on the nature of an afterlife.

That Christ actually lived and died is well recorded in Roman history. Tacitus in his *Annals*, written around the turn of the first century, explains how the burning of Rome in AD 64 was blamed by the emperor Nero on the Christians, a convenient scapegoat to cover his own infamies. Tacitus also explains why they were called Christians: "They got their name from Christ, who was executed by the sentence of the procurator Pontius Pilate in the reign of Tiberius." Tacitus was a reputable Roman historian who had little sympathy for the Christians so his writing cannot be dismissed as biased. Indeed this lack of sympathy makes it even more convincing. There is also considerable evidence in the ruins of Pompeii, destroyed by volcanic eruption in 79 AD, of Christian faith and activity.

Paul E. Little wrote in his book *Know what you Believe* that if Christ rose, we know with certainty that God exists and what he is like. The universe takes on meaning and purpose, and it is possible to experience the living God in contemporary life. On the other hand, Little says, if Christ did not rise from the dead, Christianity is an interesting museum piece, nothing more. It has no objective validity or reality. Though it is a nice wishful thought, it certainly isn't worth getting steamed up about. The martyrs who went singing to the lions in the Coliseum, and contemporary missionaries who have given their lives in Ecuador and Congo and other such places, while taking this message to others would have been poor deluded fools.

THE MOST VITAL ISSUE

The key issue about the resurrection is the empty tomb, which is pondered by Frank Morison in the title, and text, of his book, *Who Moved the Stone?* This question is important because so many attest to the fact that it had been moved; it must have been, for those witnesses to know that the tomb was empty. I have been to that garden. I have celebrated the Eucharist outside the particular tomb where Jesus is thought to have been buried. I know from my experience that it would need possibly half a dozen strong men to move the stone even with the help of a lever.

When we talk about bodily resurrection, we are talking about resurrection of the whole person, a claim made exclusively about Christianity's founder, one not made after their deaths about either Moses for Judaism, nor Mohammed for Islam.

Which makes Christianity's claim unique.

The essential argument of critics of the veracity of the resurrection of Jesus is that no one dies and rises again, therefore it could not have happened. But this ignores the power of God as creator of all life, a God whom many of the critics believe in. To suggest that God does not have that power is arrogance in the extreme.

There are four historical facts that have to be acknowledged about the resurrection. The first is that Jesus was tried by His enemies, convicted, and crucified. Second, that shortly after His burial in Joseph of Arimathea's garden, the tomb was found to be empty. Third, so many of His disciples claimed to have seen Christ alive in the flesh. Fourth, because of their conviction of what they had seen, they were inspired to start a movement that, despite persecutions and martyrdom, converted millions of people into a new way of life. This was based on His example and teachings—one of the latter, of course, reflected in the title of this work, belief in a life of a world to come.

SCEPTICAL VIEWS AND REBUTTAL

Sceptics have been advancing alternative theories for two thousand years about the resurrection, the first being that it is a myth made up by the disciples, that they expected their leader would return so they concocted the story that they saw Him alive after His death. D'Souza[50] suggests that this is the weakest argument, the idea that dead people do not come back to life is not a recent discovery, the ancient Hebrews knew that as well as we do.

Second, that Christ's Jewish followers did not expect him to come back to life, because Jews believed in bodily resurrection, but not until the end of the world, and the disciples were utterly amazed when they saw Christ in the flesh. One of them, Thomas, who was absent from the upper room when Jesus reappeared among them, when told, refused to believe them unless he was able to put his hand into Jesus' wounds.

Third, it is one thing to make up a story but quite another to be willing to endure persecution, even death, for it. Why would they be ready to die for something they knew to be a lie?

Another theory is that the disciples stole the body, but how could they have got past the soldiers, put there to guard the tomb, soldiers who knew that they would suffer imprisonment or possibly death for failing in their commission? And if the disciples had stolen the body they would have known for a fact that Christ wasn't raised from the dead, which brings us back to the problem with the previous theory; why would they have embarked upon a worldwide campaign of conversion? Why were they prepared to suffer and be put to death, for something which they knew wasn't true? All the Jewish authorities and the Roman executioners had to do to scuttle their campaign was to produce Jesus' body.

A third theory says that Christ didn't really die but was merely in a swoon or trance. This ignores the fact that Roman practice was not to take people down from the Cross who were still alive. If they were still alive at the end of the day, the time when victims were taken down, soldiers before taking them down would break the victims' legs, the shock of which would kill them almost instantly. Christ's legs were not broken, evidently because the soldiers knew Him to be dead (John 19:31–33).

The idea that Christ was merely unconscious, not dead, and revived in the tomb is farfetched, but even if He did He would have been barely conscious at the point of death, and it would be impossible to imagine a man in that condition rolling back the stone, eluding the guards, and then presenting himself to his followers.

And the disciples disconsolate over their master's death did not claim to experience a half dead man in a swoon; rather they claimed to see a man who had triumphed over death and was fully returned to life and health.

Finally there is a hallucination theory. The weakness of this argument however is that if ten people, say, report seeing something very unlikely it isn't convincing to say that they were simply dreaming or imagining things, for one has to account for them all dreaming or imagining the same thing.

D'Souza quotes the historian Gary Habermas who asks us to envision a group of people whose ship has sunk and are floating in the sea on a raft. Suddenly one man points to the horizon and cries out that he sees a ship. Sure, he may be hallucinating, but if so no one else is going to see the same ship. But if the others on the raft also see it, forget about the hallucination theory, it's time to start yelling out for help because there really is a ship out there!

And so it was with the disciples—Jesus is said to have appeared several times to them, Paul noting that more than 500 people were present on one occasion, many of whom were still alive when he wrote. James who was a sceptic about Christ being the long awaited Messiah, was only convinced after seeing his resurrected body; Thomas—the famous "doubting" Thomas—was not convinced of the resurrection until after Jesus asked him to touch His wounds. Paul, a persecutor of Christians who participated in the stoning to death of the first Christian martyr, Stephen, was not a believer until after Jesus appeared to him on the road to Damascus, which as I have suggested earlier, was his near death experience.

Jesus' death was by public execution on a cross. The government said it was for blasphemy. Jesus said it was to pay for our sin, an atonement. After He was severely tortured, Jesus' wrists and feet were nailed to a cross where He hung, eventually dying of slow suffocation. A sword was thrust into his side to confirm his death. The body of Jesus was then wrapped in linens covered with approximately 100 pounds of gummy-wet spices. His body was placed in a solid rock tomb and a huge boulder was rolled by levers to secure the entrance. Because Jesus had publicly said He would rise from the dead in three days, a guard of trained Roman soldiers was stationed at the tomb. And an official Roman seal was affixed to the tomb entrance declaring it government property.

In spite of all this, three days later the body was gone. Only the grave linens remained, in the form of the body, just lying there. The boulder formerly sealing the tomb was found up a slope, some distance away from the tomb.

WAS JESUS' RESURRECTION JUST A STORY?

The earliest explanation circulated was that the disciples stole the body. In Matthew 28:11–15, we have the record of the reaction of the chief priests and the elders when the guards gave them the infuriating and mysterious news that the body was gone. They gave the soldiers money and told them to explain that the disciples had come at night and stolen the body while they were asleep. That story was so false that Matthew didn't even bother to refute it. Testimony like this would be laughed out of any court. Furthermore, we are faced with a psychological and ethical impossibility. Stealing the body of Christ is something totally foreign to the character of the disciples and all that we know of them. It would mean that they were perpetrators of a deliberate lie which was responsible for the deception and ultimate death of thousands of people. It is inconceivable that, even if a few of the disciples had conspired and pulled off this theft, they would never have told the others.

Each of the disciples faced the test of torture and martyrdom for his statements and beliefs. Men and women will die for what they believe to be true, though it may actually be false. They do not, however, die for what they know is a lie. If ever a man or woman tells the truth, it is on their deathbed. And if the disciples had taken the body, and Christ was still dead, we would still have the problem of explaining His alleged appearances.

A second hypothesis is that the authorities, Jewish or Roman, moved the body! But why? Having put guards at the tomb, what would be their reason for moving the body? Also, what about the silence of the authorities in the face of the apostles' bold preaching about the Resurrection in Jerusalem? The ecclesiastical leaders were seething with rage, and did everything possible to prevent the spread of this message that Jesus rose from the dead. They arrested Peter and John and beat and threatened them, in an attempt to close their mouths.

But there was a very simple solution to their problem. If they had Christ's body, they could have paraded it through the streets of Jerusalem. In one fell swoop they would have successfully smothered Christianity in its cradle. That they did not do this bears eloquent testimony to the fact that they did not have the body.

Another popular theory has been that the women, distraught and overcome by grief, missed their way in the dimness of the morning and went to the wrong tomb. In their distress they imagined Christ had risen because the tomb was empty. This theory, however, falls before the same fact that destroys the previous one. If the women went to the wrong tomb, why did the high priests and other enemies of the faith not go to the right tomb and produce the body? Further, it is inconceivable that Peter and John would succumb to the same mistake, and certainly Joseph of Arimathea, owner of the tomb, would have solved the problem. In addition, it must be remembered that this was a private burial ground, not a public cemetery. There was no other tomb nearby that would have allowed them to make this mistake.

The swoon theory has also been advanced to explain the empty tomb. In this view, Christ did not actually die. He was mistakenly reported to be dead, but had swooned from exhaustion, pain, and loss of blood. When He was laid in the coolness of the tomb, He revived. He came out of the tomb and appeared to His disciples, who mistakenly thought He had risen from the dead.

This is a theory of modern construction. It first appeared at the end of the 18th century.[51] It is significant that not a suggestion of this kind has come down from antiquity among all the violent attacks which have been made on Christianity. All of the earliest records are emphatic about Jesus' death.

But let us assume for a moment that Christ was buried alive and swooned. Is it possible to believe that he would have survived three days in a damp tomb without food or water or attention of any kind? Would he have had the strength to extricate himself from the grave clothes, push the heavy stone away from the mouth of the grave, overcome the Roman guards, and walk miles on feet that had been pierced with spikes? Such a belief is more fantastic than the simple fact of the resurrection itself.

As D'Souza points out "even the German critic David Strauss who by no means believes in the Resurrection, rejected this idea as incredible." Strauss said:

> It is impossible that one who had just come forth from the grave half dead, who crept about weak and ill, who stood in the need of medical treatment, of bandaging, strengthening, and tender care, and who at last succumbed to suffering, could ever have given the disciples the impression that he was a conqueror over death and the grave; that he was the Prince of Life. Finally, if this theory is correct, Christ himself was involved in flagrant lies. His disciples believed and preached that he was dead but came alive again. Jesus did nothing to dispel this belief, rather he encouraged it.

THAT JESUS CHRIST ROSE FROM THE DEAD IS THE ONLY THEORY THAT ADEQUATELY EXPLAINS THE EMPTY TOMB

Never have so many diverse individuals on different occasions reported the same "hallucination". Hallucinations cannot account for the empty tomb, nor why the Jews and the Romans didn't settle the whole controversy by producing Jesus' body—much as they would have loved to do, the Jewish leaders to protect their religious authority over the people, the Roman executioners and guards to save face and avoid extreme punishment.

Neither the Jews nor the Romans did produce a body, because they couldn't—and, as said, a dead body never has been found.

It is difficult therefore not to agree with D'Souza that none of these alternative theories provides "even a remotely satisfactory account of the historical data before us".[52] The theories look deep, but really they are rather shallow, whereas the resurrection hypothesis, upon examination, however fanciful it seems at first, appears to provide the best possible explanation.

I cannot "prove" the truth of the resurrection, but considering the evidence objectively, I suggest that the most logical explanation for the empty tomb is that Jesus had risen.

But even accepting this, the information Jesus gives about the nature of afterlife is sparse. Therefore if we accept the "reality" of near death experiences we may turn to them to see what more detailed information we may obtain of its nature.

CHAPTER 11

The Great Hope and Christian Promise

Earlier we considered in great detail the findings of researchers world wide concerning the components of near death experiences, such as light and out-of-body experiences, their studies covering several thousand cases. This was necessary in order to establish whether there was any commonality in their findings, even as they operated independently of each other. Indeed there was, and it was most pronounced.

This commonality I suggest is a primary piece of evidence for accepting the reality of the experiences, rather than dismissing them as hallucinations and dreams; or positing biological factors put forward by sceptics, who offer no satisfactory explanation for the range of researchers who report the same pattern of components.

WHY IS THE NDE IMPORTANT?

Because some people, for whatever reason, have been given through the NDE, or other mystical experience, a glimpse of an afterlife, and have returned convinced of the reality of that experience, totally rejecting the view of many eminent medical people that there is a biological or hallucinatory explanation.

Ian's experience, quoted earlier, the simplest of all, is typical of the thousands of reports gathered from around the world in the last forty years or so, ever since Dr Moody opened up the phenomenon for serious investigation. One survey by the Gallup polling organisation in the United States in 1980, quoted in the

Journal of Near-Death Studies following this awakening of interest, suggested that more than eight million Americans had had some form of NDE.

And, I would suggest, this consistency of what experiencers report, cross-culturally, cross-nationally, and across different religious faiths is the most convincing evidence for the NDE being a "real" experience in which people do glimpse the other side and return to tell about it, rather than the alternative explanation which sceptics offer.

EARLY CHRISTIAN CHURCH BELIEF AND PRACTICE

The church, from its earliest days through to the period of the Reformation in the 16th century believed in the life of a world to come and prayed for the departed, because of the belief that they lived on in a higher intermediate realm which became known as purgatory. And before Protestants run away in horror at the very thought of that word, it is important to note its derivation, because of the pejorative sense that has grown up around it. Purgatory is from the Latin *purgo* to wash oneself, meaning nothing more than a place of spiritual cleansing and growth in preparation for higher life.

There is a neat little analogy about children at a birthday party which explains this principle well. Children are playing in the garden when the mother announces that the birthday feast is ready. The children rush to the table but she insists that they must first go and wash their hands before they are eligible to sit down at the banquet.

Unfortunately, however, so many abuses grew up in the medieval church around the concept of purgatory, and prayers and masses for the dead, that it became a major issue and in the 16th century split in the church. So much so, that praying for the dead is anathema in most non-Roman Catholic denominations today—but, fortunately, not within the particular tradition of Anglicanism from which I hail.

The principle, however, of praying for the dead had become abused by the 16th century, it having developed into a lucrative money-making venture by the Church. This needed correcting, but not the subsequent wholesale abandonment of a tradition that had been faithfully held from its earliest days.

Many see it as a classic case of throwing the baby out with the bath water.

THE KEY COMPONENTS OF NDES AND THEIR RELEVANCE TO AN AFTERLIFE

We reviewed earlier the commonality of those key components identified by various international researchers. Now, accepting the truth of an afterlife, we may look more fully at those components and determine what light they shed on the nature of that life to come.

1. Bliss:

Of all the components by far the most important for the majority of people is the overwhelming experience of great peace, even bliss, where all bodily pain they may be suffering in the earthly body disappears. So blissful, compared with this life, that they may have no desire to return.

2. Out-of-body:

The experience often begins with the person leaving his or her body, feeling weightless, and being able to look down on themselves from some objective vantage point, usually near the ceiling. Sometimes this out-of-body experience is the sum total of the experience, but it is commonplace, suggesting that those in that other life are able to look down on us, even if not us with them.

3. Departure from this world:

Being drawn rapidly through some form of dark tunnel without any apparent physical effort—the tunnel down which I started as a small boy, but didn't progress through. At the end of the tunnel they see a pinpoint of light which grows larger and larger. Usually there is no sense of fear in being drawn through the tunnel.

I find this commonly reported phenomenon particularly interesting given the fact that we come into this world drawn through a tunnel, and it is interesting to reflect that we may go out the same way.

Also, in relation to the 23rd Psalm, beloved by both Judaists and Christians, which says "though I walk through the valley of the shadow of death I fear no evil as thou art with me." For me, that description of the "valley of the shadow of death" without fear, sounds very similar to what so many report about the tunnel.

4. The light:

The fourth and most common, and for many the most significant experience, is the encounter with the light, the subject of Chapter 7. Nearly always it is described as white or golden, very brilliant, but not dazzling, which does not hurt the eyes, and here I draw your attention again to Ian's encounter and description:

> I knew I was going "there" walking toward the "sun" which drew me toward it with its inviting glow and warmth. The most delightful yellowish colour imaginable across the clean clear blue green water.

Often the light is identified as a being. If the person is religious, this may be an obvious religious figure such as Jesus, or simply a presence which is felt to be God or God-like. This is nearly always such an intensely emotional experience, that experiencers cannot find words to describe their feelings—it is ineffable. But the experience of the being of light is always a positive one, described as warm, welcoming, and loving unconditionally.

5. A barrier:

Often people report some form of barrier, a wall, a gate, a fence or, as in the case of Ian, a blue green lagoon between him and the light, or even just a feeling that they are at a point beyond which they cannot pass. It seems to be a point of no return, for there is an awareness that if crossed they cannot come back.

Jesus' story about the afterlife, involving Dives and Lazarus, makes it clear that once this barrier is finally crossed there can be no return.

6. Another country:

A visit to, or a glimpse of, another country is often reported, usually an idyllic pastoral scene, brilliantly coloured and filled with light.

7. Meeting loved ones:

At funerals I always make the point about the life to come that if God is love, the only satisfactory description made of him, then the most loving thing he could do for us when we cross over is grant us reunion on that other shore with those who have gone before whom we loved in this life.

Many people report meeting and talking with loved ones, relatives, or friends who had previously died. In some instances these people beckon to them eagerly, but at other times wave them away, albeit lovingly, signalling that they should go back. The phrase “it is not your time yet”, or similar, is common.

8. A life review:

Particularly interesting because the nature of the life review is not at all judgmental as one might expect.

The life review is only judgmental in the sense of one being invited to sit in self-judgement. In the review one is shown the effects of one’s words and actions on other people. This is particularly important in relation to those who have to return to this life, and invariably it produces a complete change in attitude towards others. Dr Eben Alexander is an excellent example.

Some also have a preview of events in their future for which they must return to their earthly life to complete certain tasks.

9. A point of decision:

Remember how Ian spoke of the point of decision when he wondered, “Was I to walk on the water” followed by an immediate return to his body on the operating table. In his case it doesn’t appear that he had to make a decision, it was made for him. Whereas Father Neuhaus was given the option of continuing on in this life, or moving to the higher realm

More often than not people want to stay in this new life dimension that they have glimpsed, but they realise that this is impossible, that they have responsibilities, usually family, which they must return to and meet. Sometimes they are given the opportunity themselves to make the decision to go back and, in fact, choose to do so, but others are sent back by the being of light or by the friends or relatives they have met. They return with a sense of unfinished business which they must complete before they are finally allowed to "cross the barrier".

10. The return:

The return to the body is usually rapid, often reported as shooting backwards down the tunnel at great speed, or a sense of being snapped back into the body.

11. The aftermath:

For most people the NDE is the most profound experience they will ever have. It is vividly remembered for years, often for a whole lifetime. This conviction of vividness and reality is accompanied by a loss of all fear of death. Again Ian was typical in this regard.

> I know we need not fear death but can look forward to it! I am able to tell people close to death "welcome it, it's going to be the best experience ever!" I can now tell those grieving the death of another . . . "rejoice".

People don't say that they want to die, but that they will have no fear when they have to. Indeed not only do they not say they want to die but they say they have a renewed sense of value and purpose in this life, and often they discover they have returned with great healing and psychic powers. If they have some form of religious faith their experience tends to confirm and strengthen that faith. Even if they have no faith they return to this life convinced that death to this life is not the end.

CONCLUSION

I believe, as D'Souza has so well articulated,[53] that human life is probably the most exciting romantic adventure in the universe, going on stage after stage, and yet most people pass into the unseen "as stupidly as a caterpillar on a cabbage leaf" without curiosity or joy or wonder or excitement at the boundless career ahead.

He asks: What is the matter with us today? Have we lost the faith of our forebears of earlier days? Have we been blinded by the so-called enlightenment and technological progress of the 20th and 21st centuries?

Instead of the thrill of adventure we have the dull grey monotony of aged lives drawing near their close, and the loneliness of parting is intensified in the hearts of the bereaved as the beloved one crosses the barrier.

To this I would add that fortunately we have today the evidence of near death experiences which suggest in the strongest terms that death is not the end. God, if you believe in God, did not create us just to destroy us, and a new plane of existence awaits that is even more exciting, stimulating, and wonderful.

Like the baby in the womb we fear the unknown, but just as we know from our own experience that babies should not fear what is unknown to them, we have much evidence to suggest neither should we fear the next stage of our existence. Indeed, we should look forward to it eagerly, which is exactly what we would tell the baby in the womb were we able to communicate. Part of that evidence, I suggest, is the near death experience.

The great Promise? You will hear it at every Christian funeral service you may ever attend (John 14:2–3):

> In my Father's house there are many mansions—I go to prepare a place for you.
>
> And if I go and prepare a place for you I will come again and receive you unto myself; that where I am there you may be also.

NOTES

1 For details see 1 Corinthians 15.
2 Matthew 17:1–9, Mark 9:2–8, Luke 9:28–36.
3 Bowker; *The Oxford Dictionary of World Religions*; p.27.
4 Ibid.
5 Ibid.: p.28.
6 Ibid.
7 Welcome and Mission Statement of "Got Atheism". See: GotAtheism.dot.com <http.://GotAtheism.dot.com>, 2009.
8 D'Souza, D.; *Life after Death*; D'Souza website: dineshdsouza.com <http.://dineshdsouza.com>, ygodinstitute.org <http://ygodinstitute.org>.
9 Fosdick, H.E.; *The Assurance of Immortality*; 1958; p.59ff.
10 Ibid.: p.65.
11 Letter in Yale Library, dated 9 March 1790.
12 Papini, G.; *The Story of Christ*; p.410.
13 Fosdick, H.E.; *The Assurance of Immortality*; p.59ff.
14 Teyrovsky, G.; *Journal of Near-Death Studies*; Vol. 30, no. 4, 2011; p.13.
15 Moody, R.; *Life after Life*.
16 Near death experiencers.
17 IANDS Home Page statement.
18 *Lancet*, 2001; no. 358; pp. 2039–45.
19 Mitchell, C.; *Near Death—Stories from the Other Side*; Mandarin, Reed Books, Melbourne; 1996.
20 My experience as a small boy—see chapter 1.
21 Atwater, P.; *Beyond the Light*; Alpha Books; 2000.
22 Jowett, B. (translator); *Essential Plato, "The Republic"*; Softback Preview; 1999; p.407ff.
23 Furniss, John; *The Sight of Hell*.
24 *The Oxford Dictionary of the Christian Church*; Julian of Norwich, p.753.
25 Atwater, P.; *Beyond the Light*; paperback version; p.23ff.
26 Storm, Howard; *My Descent into Death—A Second Chance at Life*; Doubleday, New York; 2005.

27 <http://www.youtube.com/watch?v=4H-4JVpAIAI> .
28 Ritchie, J.; *Death's Door: True Stories of Near Death Experiences.*
29 Ring, Kenneth; *Heading towards Omega.*
30 Amazon.com/To-Heaven-Back-DoctorsExtraordinary/dp/0307731715. Q & A with Mary C. Neal, M.D.
31 *Journal of Near-Death Studies*; Vol. 3, 2003.
32 IANDS Archives, www.iands.org/ndes/nde-stories/iands-nde-accounts.html
33 Ibid.
34 Tribbe, Frank C.; *Portrait of Jesus?*; Stein and Day, New York; 1983; p.245.
35 Alexander, Eben; *Proof of Heaven—A Neurosurgeon's Journey into the Afterlife*; Pan Macmillan, Sydney; 2013; p.8ff.
36 *IANDS Vital Signs*; Vol. 21, no. 2, 2002; p.3.
37 A much misunderstood doctrine, particularly by Protestants who see it as a pejorative term, whereas it derives from the simple Latin word *purgo*—to cleanse oneself—hence purgatory is a place of spiritual cleansing.
38 MacGregor, G.; *The Nicene Creed*; Wm. B. Eerdmans, Grand Rapids, Michigan; 1980; p.xi.
39 Spooner, J.; *The Archbishops of Railway Square*; Halstead Press, Sydney; 2002; p.29.
40 Acts 22:6–16; 26:12–18.
41 Atwater, P.; *Beyond the Light*; Avon Books, New York; 1994; p.12.
42 Bread 6:35; Light 8:12; Gate 10:9; Good Shepherd 10:11; Way, Truth, Life 14:6; True Vine.
43 Teyrovsky, G.; *Journal of Near Death Studies*; Vol. 30, no. 4, 2011; p.13.
44 Carter, C.; *Science and the Near-Death Experience.*
45 Fenwick, P.; *The Truth in the Light*; p.308.
46 D'Souza; *Life after Death*; p.66.
47 *Lancet*; 358, no. 9298 (2001); "NDEs in Survivors of Cardiac Arrest"; p.2039–45.
48 *Lancet*, 2001; no. 358; pp. 2039–45.
49 D'Souza, ibid.: p.224.
50 According to D'Souza, *Life after Death.*
51 Ibid.: p.227.
52 Ibid.

ACKNOWLEDGEMENTS

First and foremost I must thank Dr. Adrienne Hall without whose independent research, encouragement, patience, and sound guidance over a long period of time I could never have reached this stage of publication.

I am also indebted to certain fellow members of the International Association for Near-Death Studies (IANDS), of which I have been a member for more than twenty years, for a major contribution in the preparation of this book. I also thank my niece Stephanie Trainer for her excellent (voluntary) editing.

An essential for me was to able to show that a series of researchers, cross-culturally, cross-nationally, and independently of one another, who instituted their own studies, prompted by the lead of Dr. Raymond Moody in his work *Life After Life* in 1975, investigating the "reality" and composition of components in near death experiences.

Their studies I drew on extensively allowing me to show the considerable commonality in the pattern of several thousand near death experiencers.

Establishing this commonality was an essential element in making my case for the "reality" of the experiences, and I could only do this by drawing upon these independent findings. Approaching 90 years of age this research was a task impossible to do for myself!

First was the ground-breaking work of Raymond Moody, who set in train, through his example, the series of independent studies by other researchers.

Others whom I quoted from and whom I wish acknowledge, whose works may be found in the Bibliography at the end of this book, and are highly recommended reading, include Dr Peter Fenwick for his research in England; Dr. Pim van Lommel in the Netherlands; Dr. David San Filippo in Florida; Craig Mitchell in Australia; Dr. Jeffrey Long in Louisiana; a Tibetan Buddhist quoted by Kevin Williams on an NDE website; and finally, for Dr. P.M.H. Atwater for the value of her findings through her own near death experiences, and the sheer volume of others interviewed by her.

In developing my story I am particularly grateful for the insights I received from Dinesh D'Souza in his works *Life After Death* and *What's so Great about Christianity*.

With thanks to all: the Revd John Spooner

BIBLIOGRAPHY

Alexander, Eben; *Proof of Heaven—A Neurosurgeon's Journey into the Afterlife*; Pan Macmillan, Sydney; 2013.

Atwater, P.H.; *Coming Back to Life*; Ballantine Books, New York; 1988.

Atwater, P.H.; *The Complete Idiot's Guide to Near Death Experiences;* Alpha Books, Macmillan USA; 2000.

Aurelio, John R.; *Returnings; Life after Death Experience, a Christian View*; The Continuum Publishing Company, New York; 1999.

Bain, B.; *Divine Encounters—Near Death Experiences in Retrospect*; 1999.

Baker, Rt Revd John Austin; *Evidence for the Resurrection*; Mowbray for The Christian Evidence Society, Oxford; 1986.

Barrett, Sir William; *Death Bed Visions*; Psychic Press; 1926; Reprint: Hurricane, Florida; 1986.

Barton, John; *Love Unknown: Meditations on the Death and Resurrection of Jesus*; SPCK, London; 1990.

Boer, H.R.; *A Short History of the Early Church*; Wm. B. Eerdmans Publishing Company, Grand Rapids, Michigan; 1976.

Bowker, John (editor); *Oxford Dictionary of World Religions*; Oxford University Press, Oxford; 1997.

Brinkley, Dannion with Perry, Paul; *Saved by the Light*; Judy Piatkus, London; 1994.

Browning, W.R.F.; *Oxford Dictionary of the Bible*; Oxford University Press, Oxford; 1996.

Brundrit, D.F.; *Is the Resurrection True?*; Phillip Allan, London; 1934.

Burpo, Todd; *Heaven is for Real;* Thomas Nelson, Nashville; 2010.

Callanan, M. and Kelly, P; *Final Gifts; Understanding the Special Awareness, Needs, and Communications of the Dying*; Bantam Books, New York; 1997.

Chadwick, H.; *The Early Church*; Penguin Books, Harmondsworth, England; 1977.

Dowding, Air Chief Marshall Lord; *Many Mansions*; Rider, London; 1956.

Drolma D; *Journey to Realms Beyond Death;* Padma Publishing, Junction City, California; Mandala for 1999.

D'Souza, Dinesh; *Life after Death—The Evidence*; Regency Publishing,Washington; 2009.

Eby, Richard E.; *Caught up into Paradise; A Physician's Amazing Account*; Baker Book House, Grand Rapids, Michigan; 1978.

Elder, Bruce; *And When I Die Will I be Dead?*; Compiled from the ABC Radio documentary of that name; ABC Enterprises, Sydney; 1987.

Emrich, Rt Revd Richard S.; *Death and Hope*; First published by the Diocese of Michigan, revised and reprinted by Forward Movement Publications.

Fenwick, Peter and Elizabeth; *The Truth in the Light: An Investigation of Over 300 Near Death Experiences*; BCA, London; 1995.

Fosdick, H.E.; *The Assurance of Immortality*; James Clarke, London; 1958.

Gallup, George; *Adventures in Immortality*.

Gill, Derek; *Quest: The Life of Elisabeth Kubler-Ross*; Harper and Row, New York; 1981.

Gordon, David Cole; *Overcoming the Fear of Death*; Penguin Books, Baltimore; 1970.

Gordon, Margot; *Return From Death*; Arkana, London; 1985.

Guggenheim, B. & J.; *Hello from Heaven: A New Field of Research Confirms that Life and Love are Eternal*; Longwood, Florida: The ADC Project; 1995.

Holy Bible; The New Revised Standard Version; Thomas Nelson, Nashville, Tennessee; 1989. Ezekiel 1 and 2; Isaiah 6; Mark 1: 9–13; Acts 9: 1–30; 2 Corinthians 12: 1–7; Daniel.

Inglis, Brian; *Life after Death*; Orbis Publishing, London; 1984.

James, William; *Varieties of Religious Experience*; JWS. Described by Andrew Greeley in the foreword to Moody's 'The Light Beyond' as "perhaps America's greatest thinker".

Jung, Carl; *Memories, Dreams, Reflections*.

Kellehear, Allan; *Experiences Near Death; Beyond Medicine & Religion*. Attacks religious attitudes to NDEs; examines NDEs in different cultures.

Kelly, J.N.D.; *Early Christian Doctrines*; Adam and Charles Black, London; 1958.

Keneally, Thomas; *Schindler's Ark*. Supposed to have been as given in approximately 1,000 notarised documents by Jewish survivors.

Kircher, P.M.; *Love is the Link: A Hospice Doctor Shares her Experiences with Near Death and Dying*; Larson Publications, New York; 1995.

Klinkenborg, V.; *At the Edge of Eternity*; Life Magazine, March,1992, p.65/73.

Kubler-Ross, Elisabeth; *On Death and Dying*; Collier Books, New York; 1969.

Kubler-Ross, Elisabeth; *On Death and Dying*; Macmillan Publications, New York; 1997.

Kubler-Ross, Elisabeth; *Questions and Answers on Death and Dying*; Collier Books, New York; 1974.

Kubler-Ross, Elisabeth; *Death: The Final Stage of Growth*; Prentice -Hall Inc.; Englewood Cliffs, New Jersey; 1975.

Kubler-Ross, Elisabeth; *The Wheel of Life*; Bantam Press, New York; 1997.

Lewis, C.S.; *Chronicles of Narnia; The Last Battle*. Ch13, "How the Dwarfs Refused to be Taken in", is a story of how attitudes shape spiritual experience.

Little, Paul E.; *Beyond Blind Faith*.

Malz, Betty; *My Glimpse of Eternity*; Baker Book House, Grand Rapids, Michigan; 1994.

Markus, R.A.; *Christianity in the Roman World*; Thames and Hudson, London; 1974.

Moody, Raymond; *Life after Life*; Bantam Books, New York; 1975.

Moody, Raymond; *Reflections on Life after Life*; Bantam Books, New York; 1977.

Moody, Raymond; *Reunion; Visionary Encounters with Departed Loved Ones*; Little Brown and Company, London; 1994.

Moody, Raymond; *The Light Beyond*; Bantam Books, New York; 1989.

Morison, F.; *Who Moved the Stone?*; Faber and Faber, London; 1958.

Neal, Mary; *To Heaven and Back*; Waterbrook Multnomah, New York; 2012.

Neuhaus, Fr. Richard John; *Vital Signs*; Vol. 21, 2, 2002.

Osis, Karlis and Erendur; *At the Hour of Death*; Avon Books, New York; 1977.

Papini, Giovanni; *The Story of Christ*; Hodder and Stoughton, London; 1923.

Piper, Don; *90 Minutes in Heaven*; Revell, Grand Rapids, Michigan; 2004.

Pittenger, Norman; *After Death; Life in God*; SCM Press, London; 1980.

Quick, O.C.; *Doctrines of the Creed*; James Nisbet.

Randles, Jenny and Hough, Peter; *Life after Death and the World Beyond*; Piatkus, London; 1996.

Richards, H.J.; *The First Easter: What Really Happened?*; Mowbray, Oxford; 1972.

Richards, H.J.; *Death and After: What Really Will Happen?*; Mowbray, London and Oxford; 1986.

Ring, Kenneth; *Heading towards Omega*; William Morrow; 1984.

Ring, Kenneth; *Lessons from the Light*; Plenum Publishing Corporation, New York; 1998.

Ring, Kenneth; *Life after Death*; Quill, New York; 1980.

Rinpoche, Sogyal; *The Tibetan Book of Living and Dying*; Harper Collins, San Francisco; 1982.

Roberts, A. and Donaldson, J. (editors); *The Anti-Nicene Fathers; Translations of the Fathers down to AD325*; Vol. 1; Wm. B. Eeerdmans, Grand Rapids, Michigan; 1985.

Sabom, Michael; *Recollections of Death*; Corgi Books, London; 1982.

Sherman, Harold; *The Dead are Alive*; Fawcett Gold Medal, New York; 1981.

Spooner, J.; *The Archbishops of Railway Square: A History of Christ Church, St. Laurence Sydney*; Halstead Press, Sydney; 2002.

Stevenson, J.; *A New Eusebius; Documents Illustrative of the History of the Church to AD 337*; S.P.C.K, London; 1957.

Sutcliffe, J.M.; *A Dictionary of Religious Education*; SC Book; 1984.

Vincent, Ken R.; *Visions of God; From the Near Death Experience*; Larson Publications.

Walker, W.; *A History of the Christian Church*; T. and T. Clark, Edinburgh; 4th Edition, 1986.

Wambach, Helen; *Life before Life*; Bantam Books, New York; 1979.

Wills-Brandon, C.; *One Last Hug Before I Go: The Mystery and Meaning of Deathbed Visions*; Health Communications; 2000.

Winter, David; *Evidence for Life after Death*; Mowbray for Christian Evidence Society, London; 1989.

Winter, David; *Hereafter*; Date—c.1973.

Zaleski, Carol; *Otherworld Journeys; Accounts of Near death Experiences in Medieval and Modern Times*; Oxford University Press, New York; 1987.